MAGNI*FL*YING GLASS

&

KOOKY COLORING BOOK

MAGNIFLYING GLASS
Coloring Book

A Completely Random Adventure in Coloring Book World

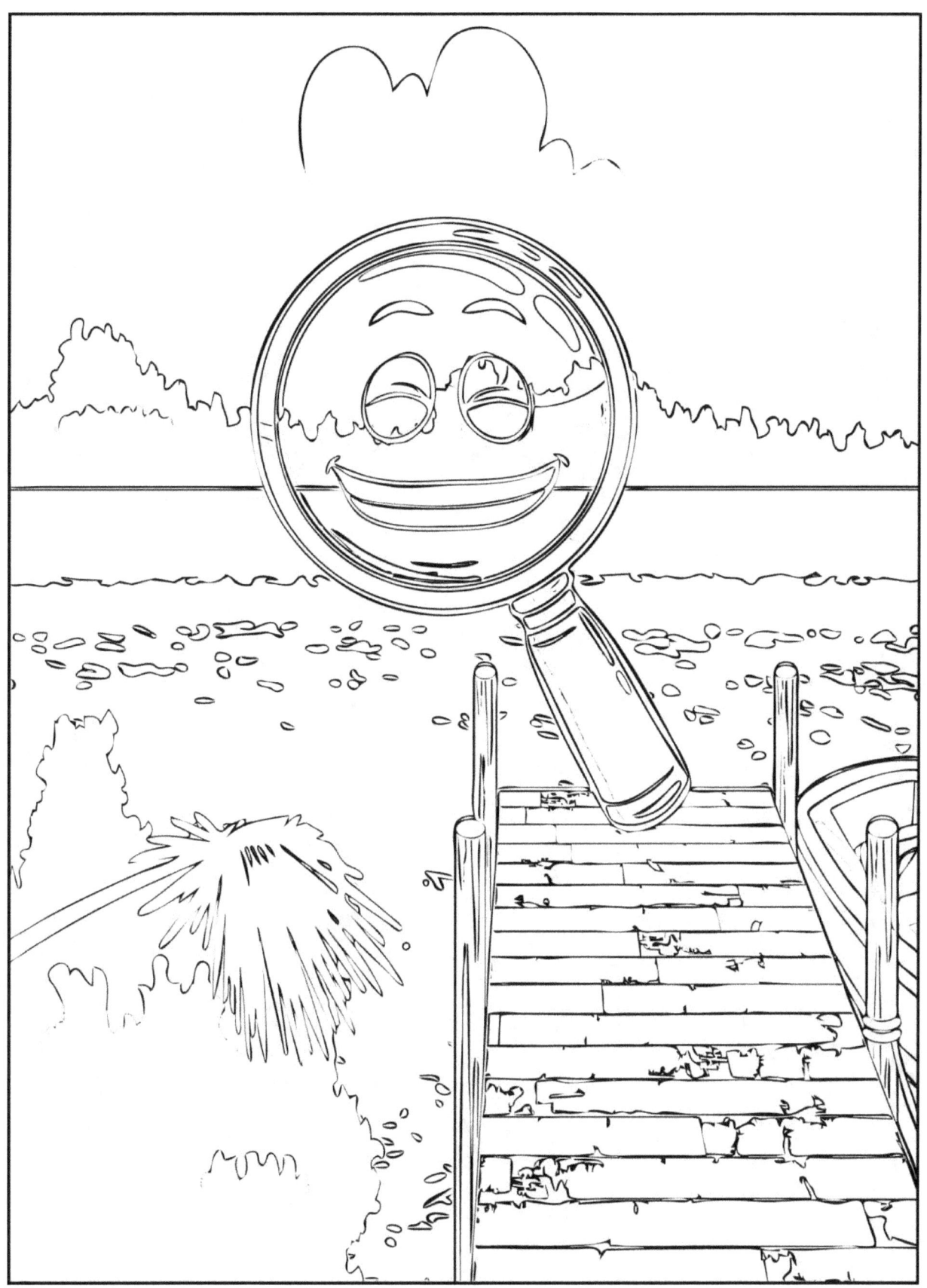

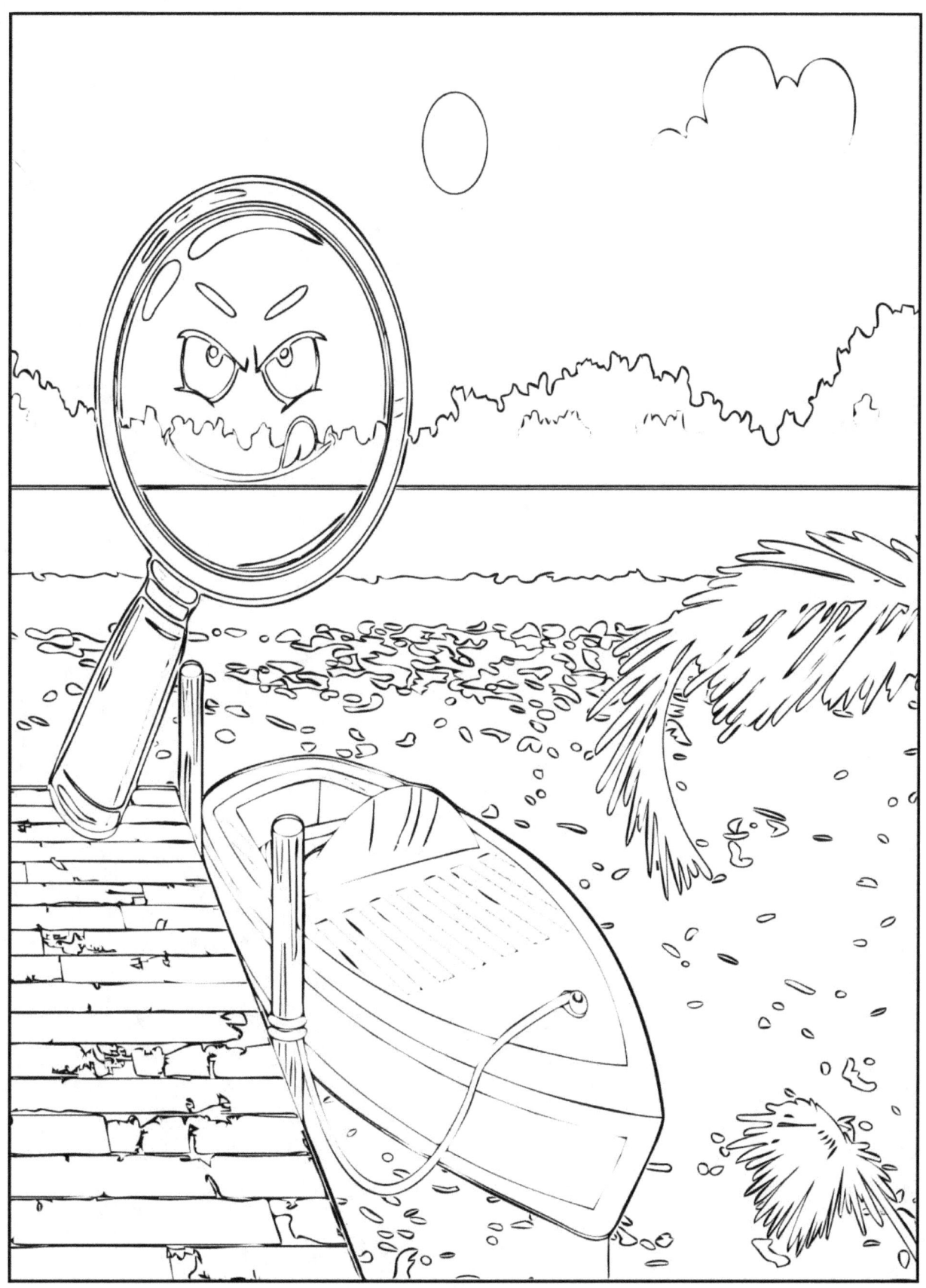

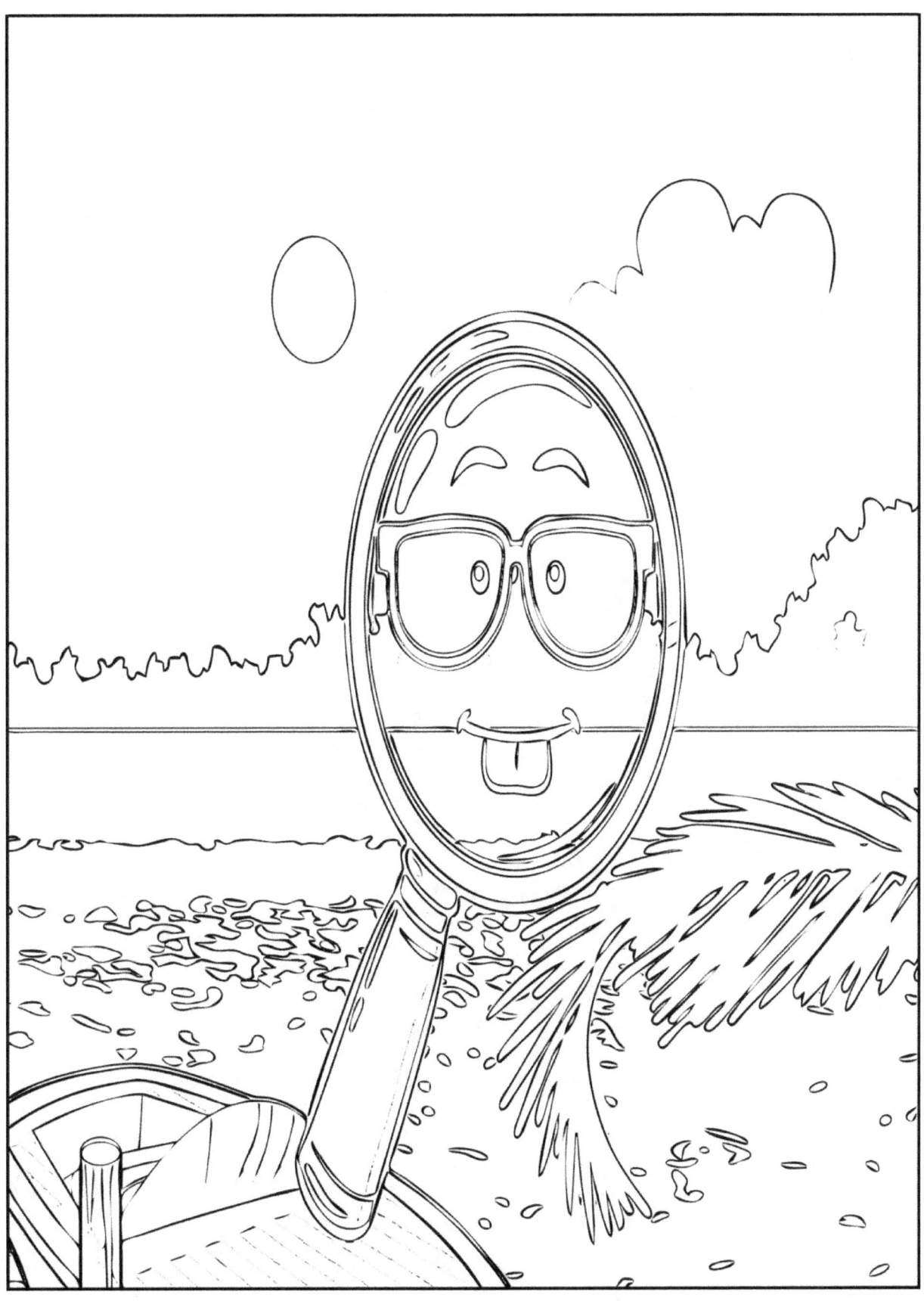

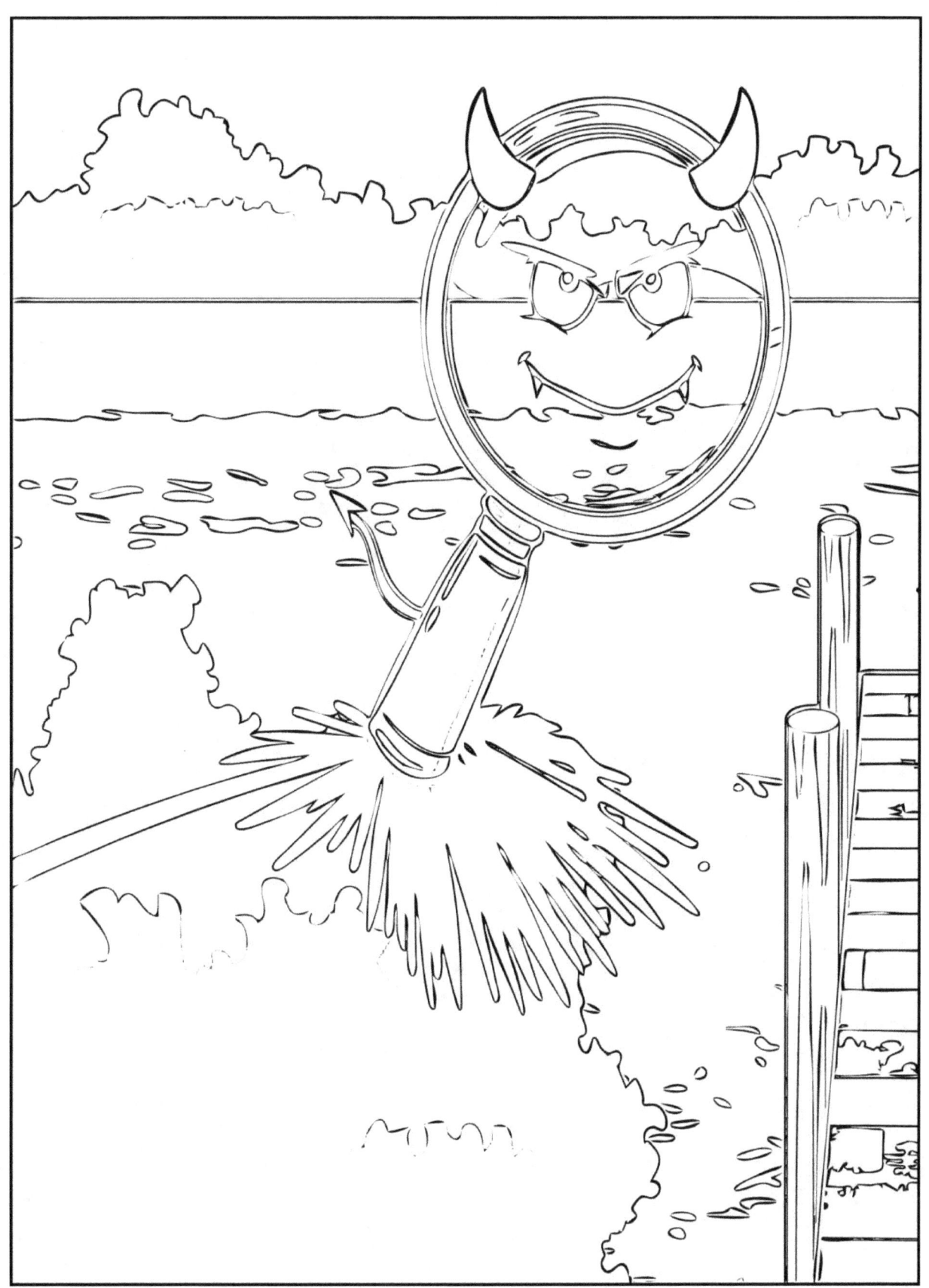

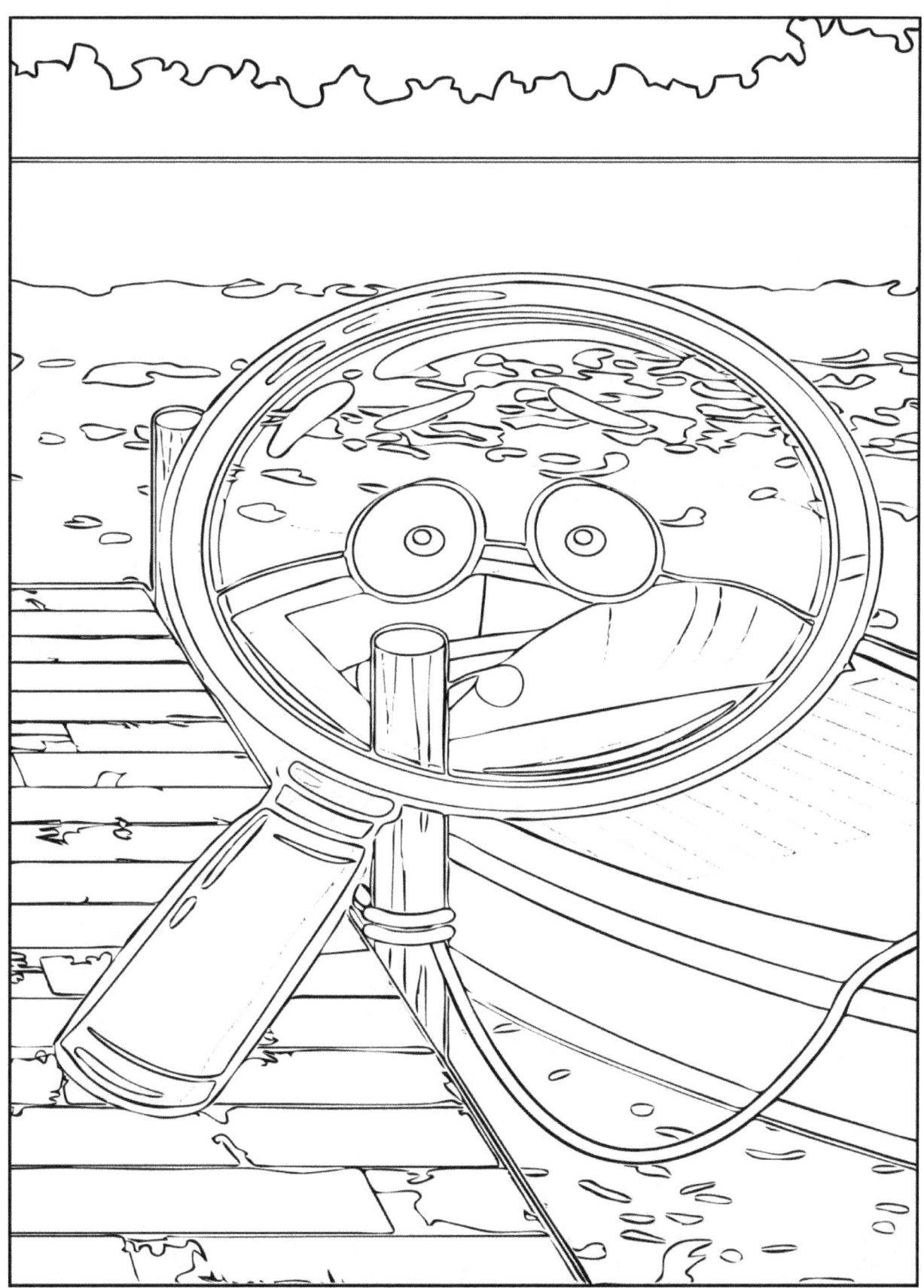

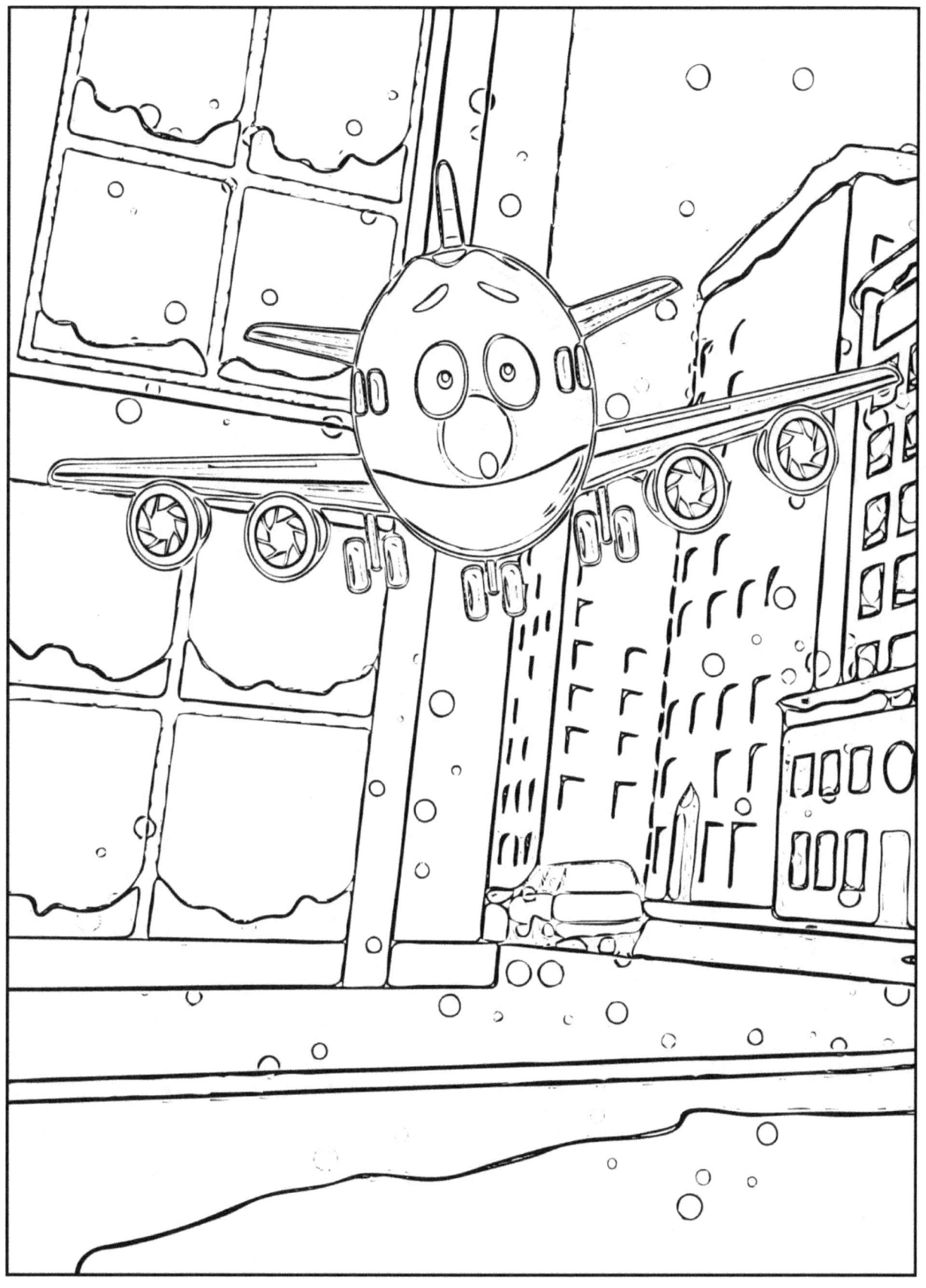

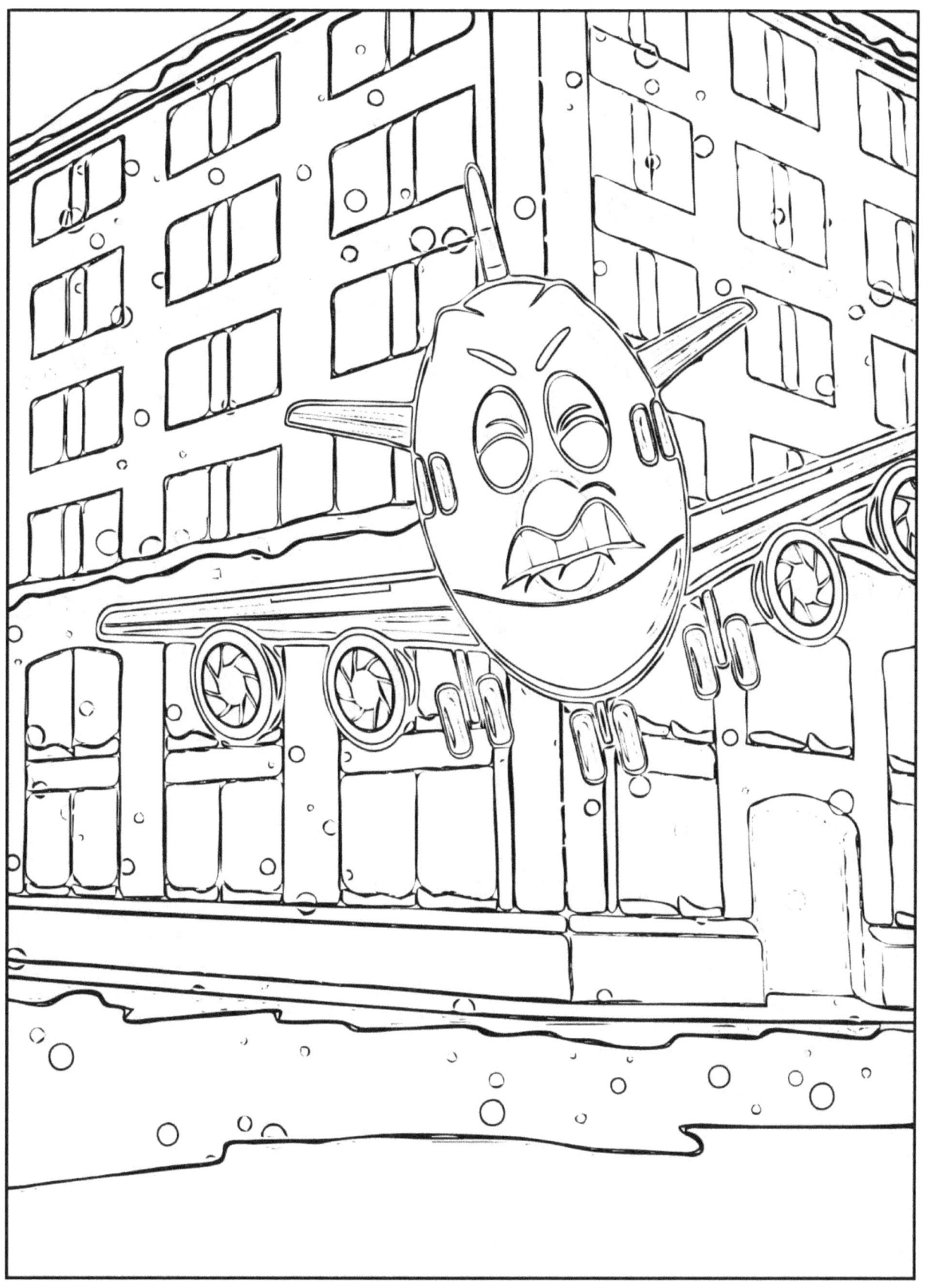

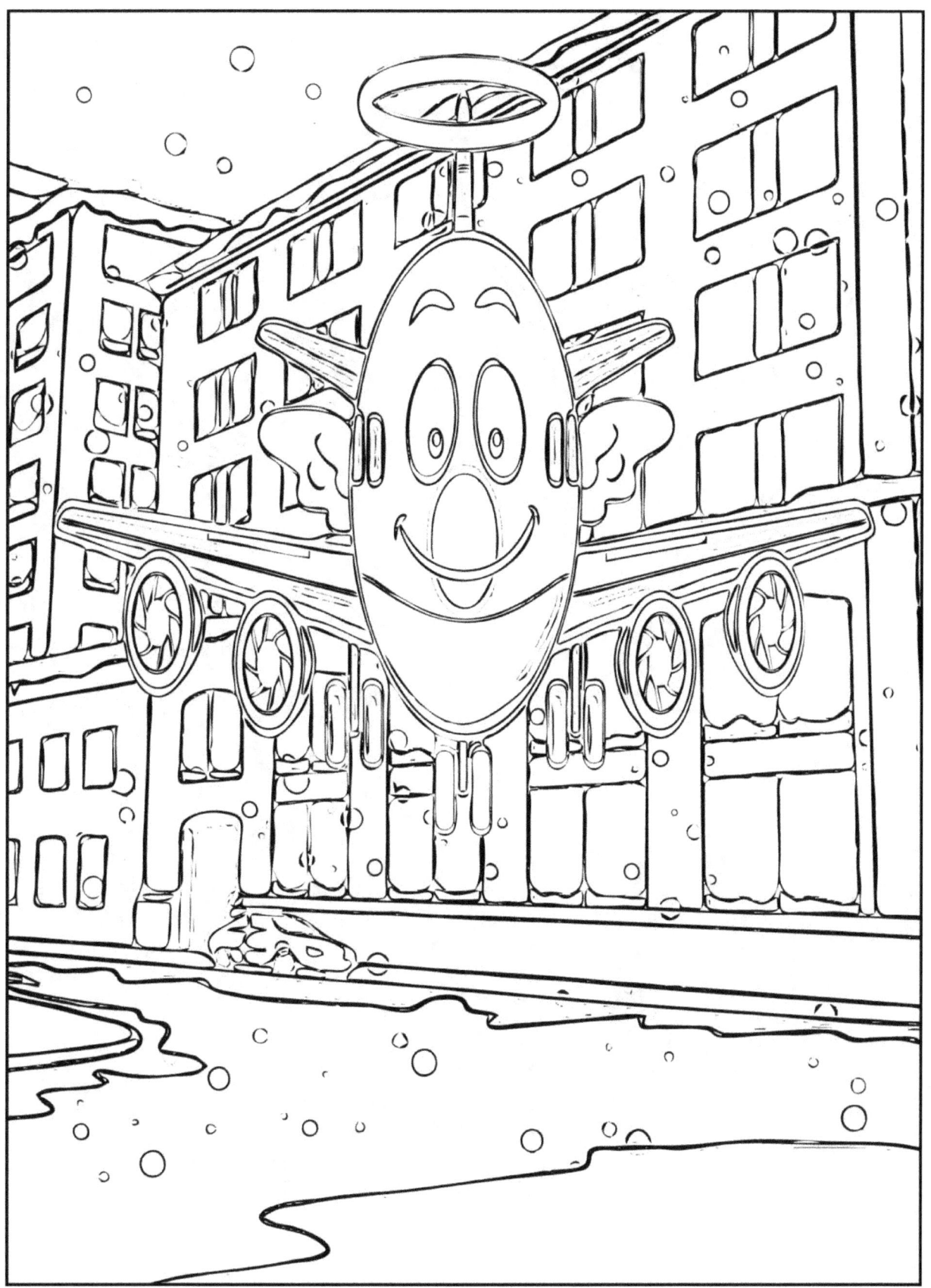

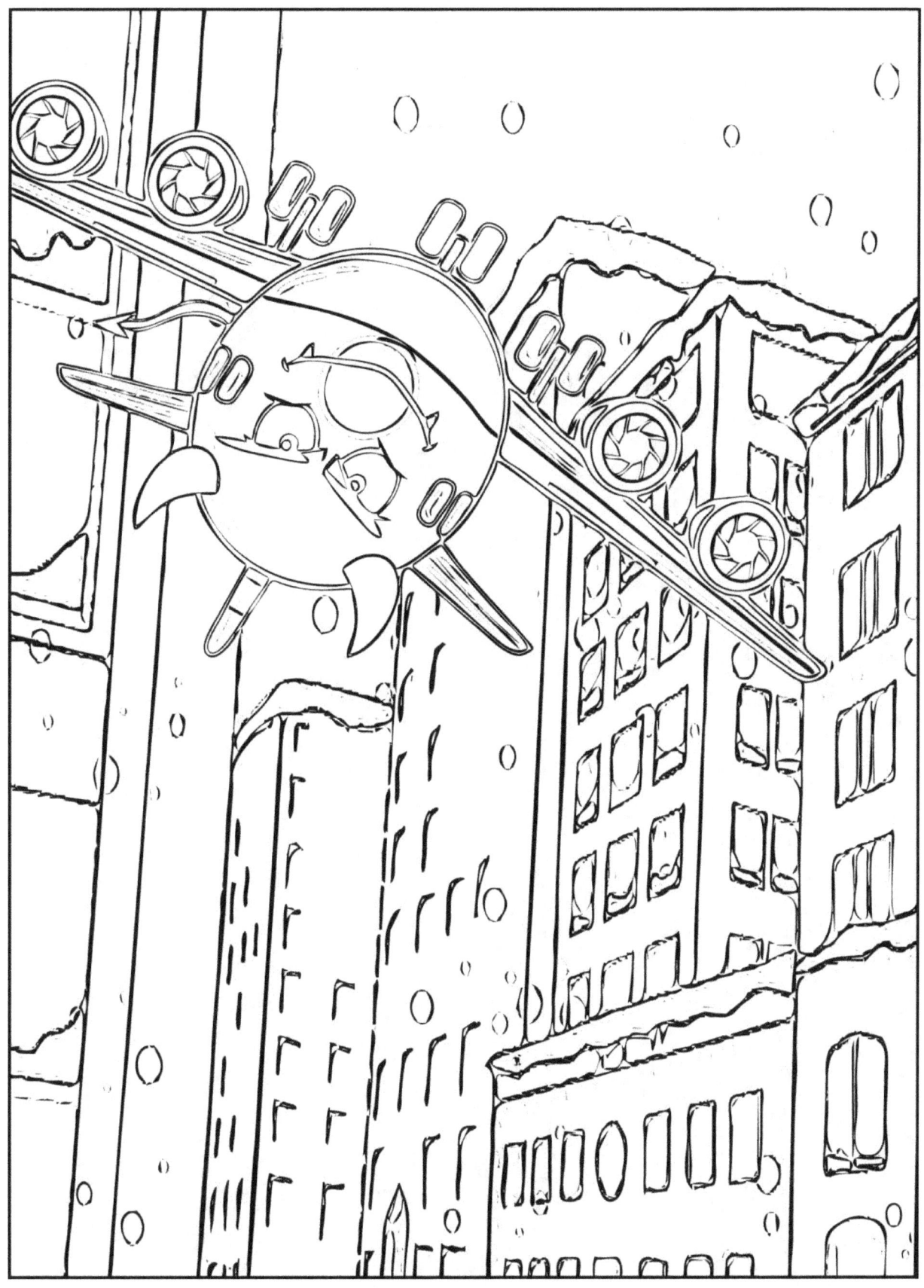

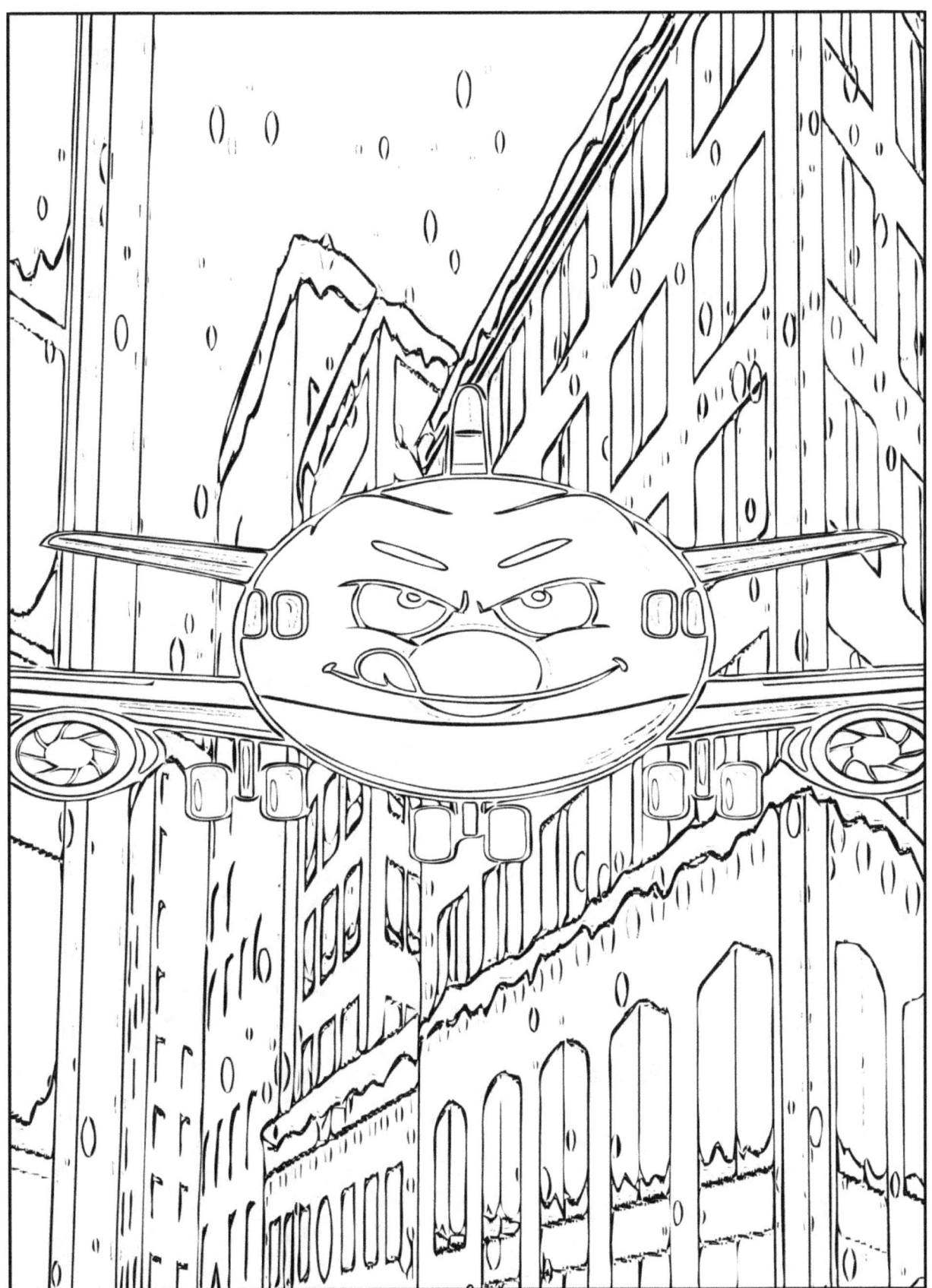

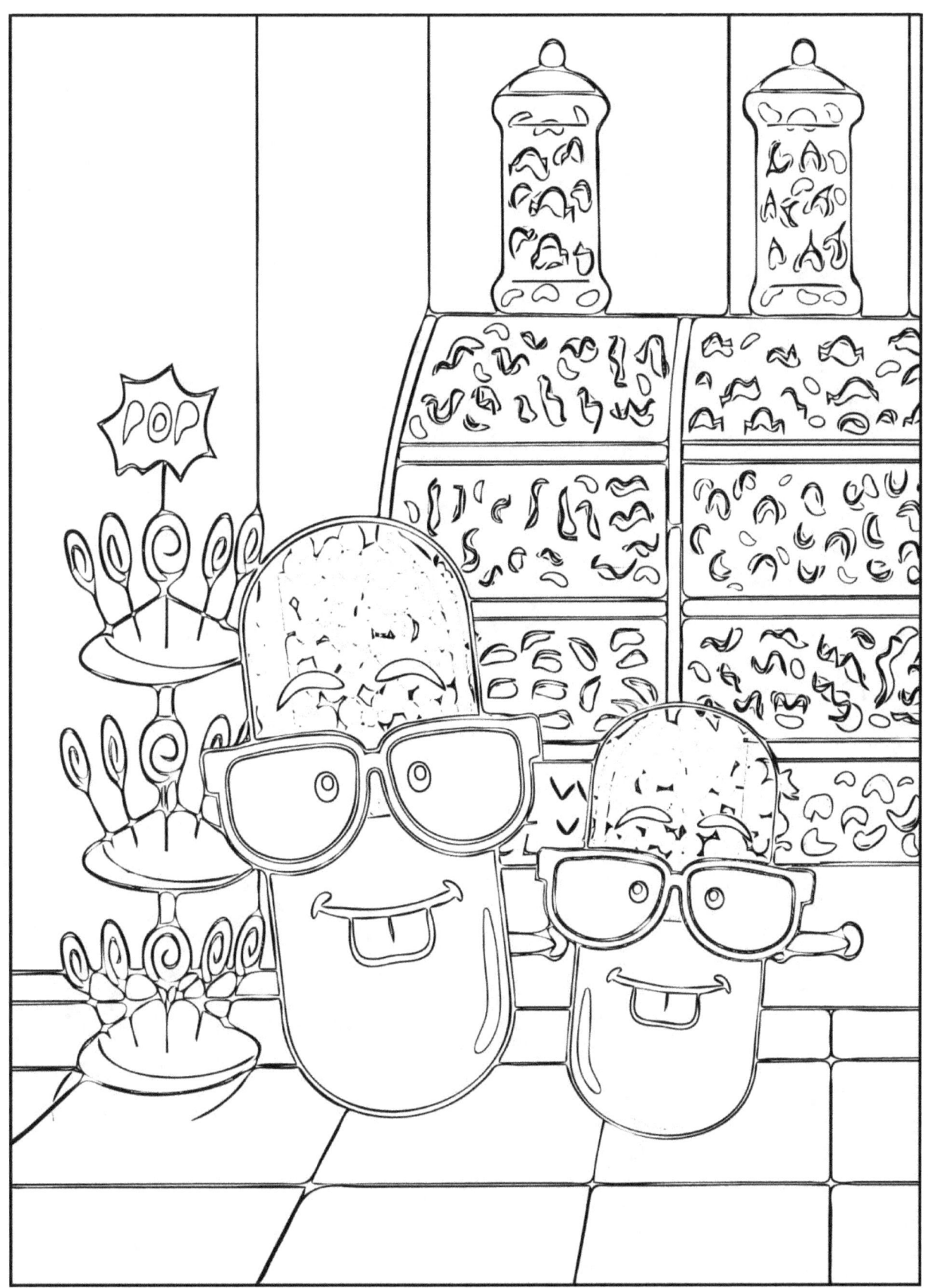

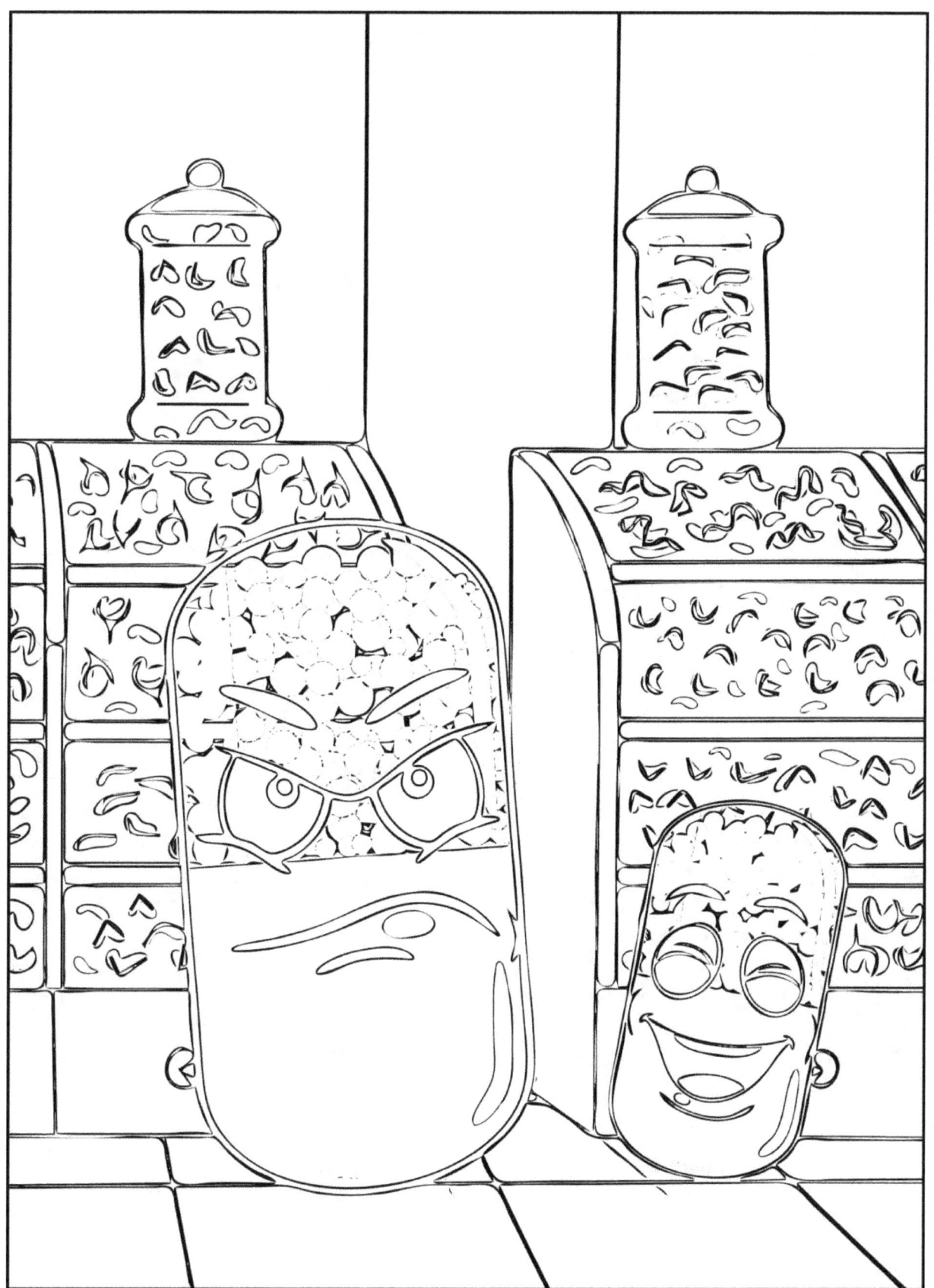

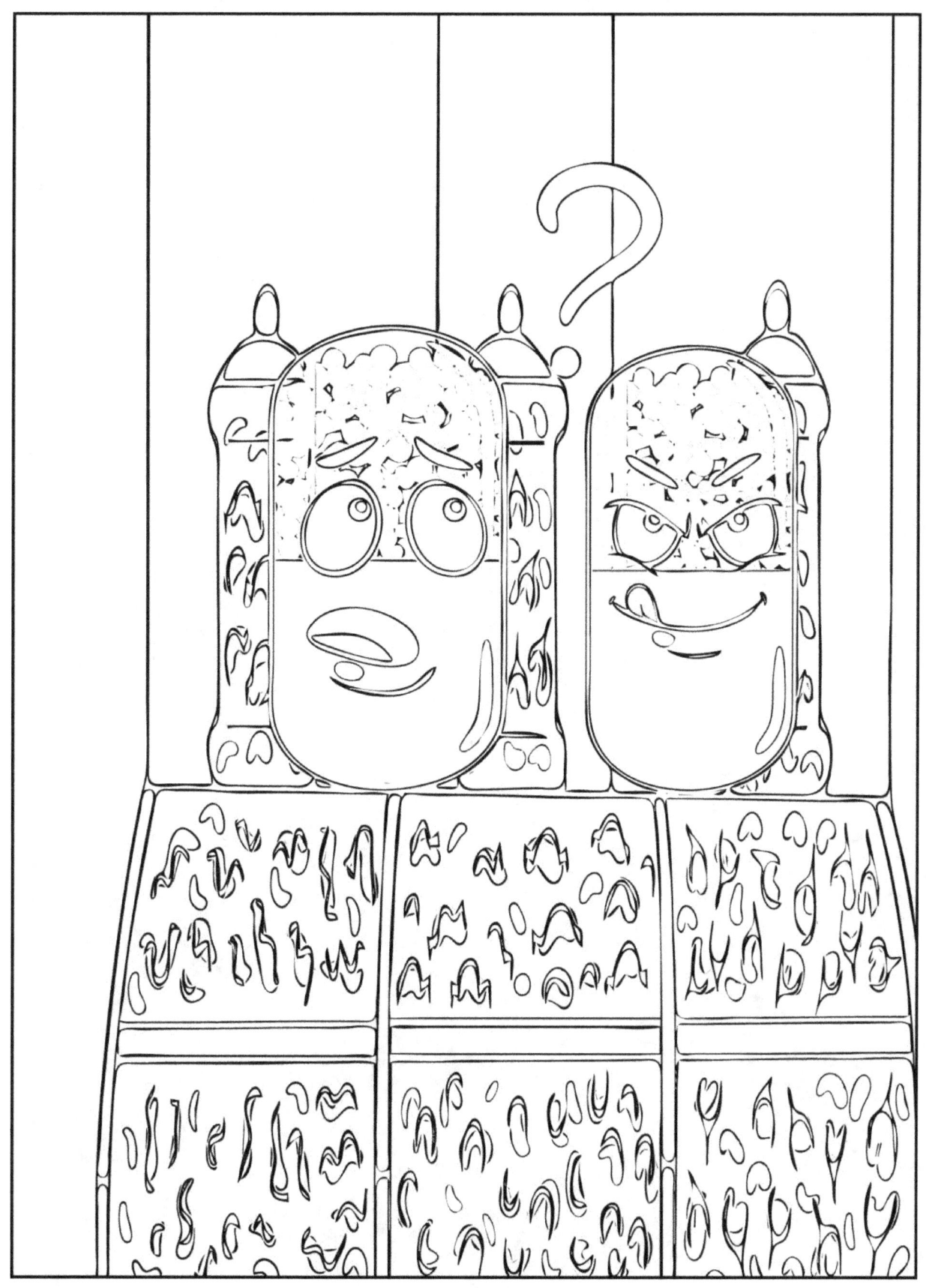

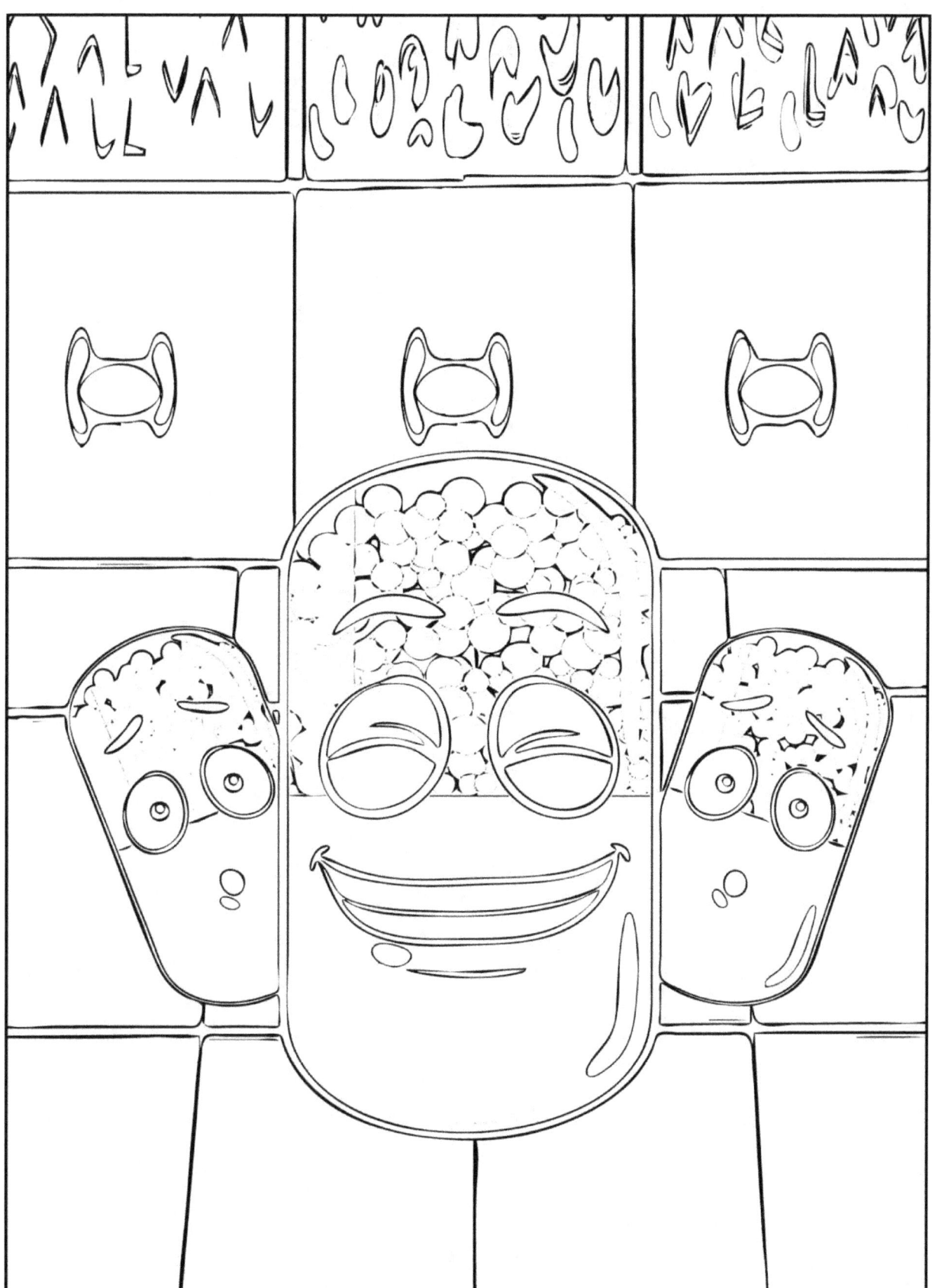

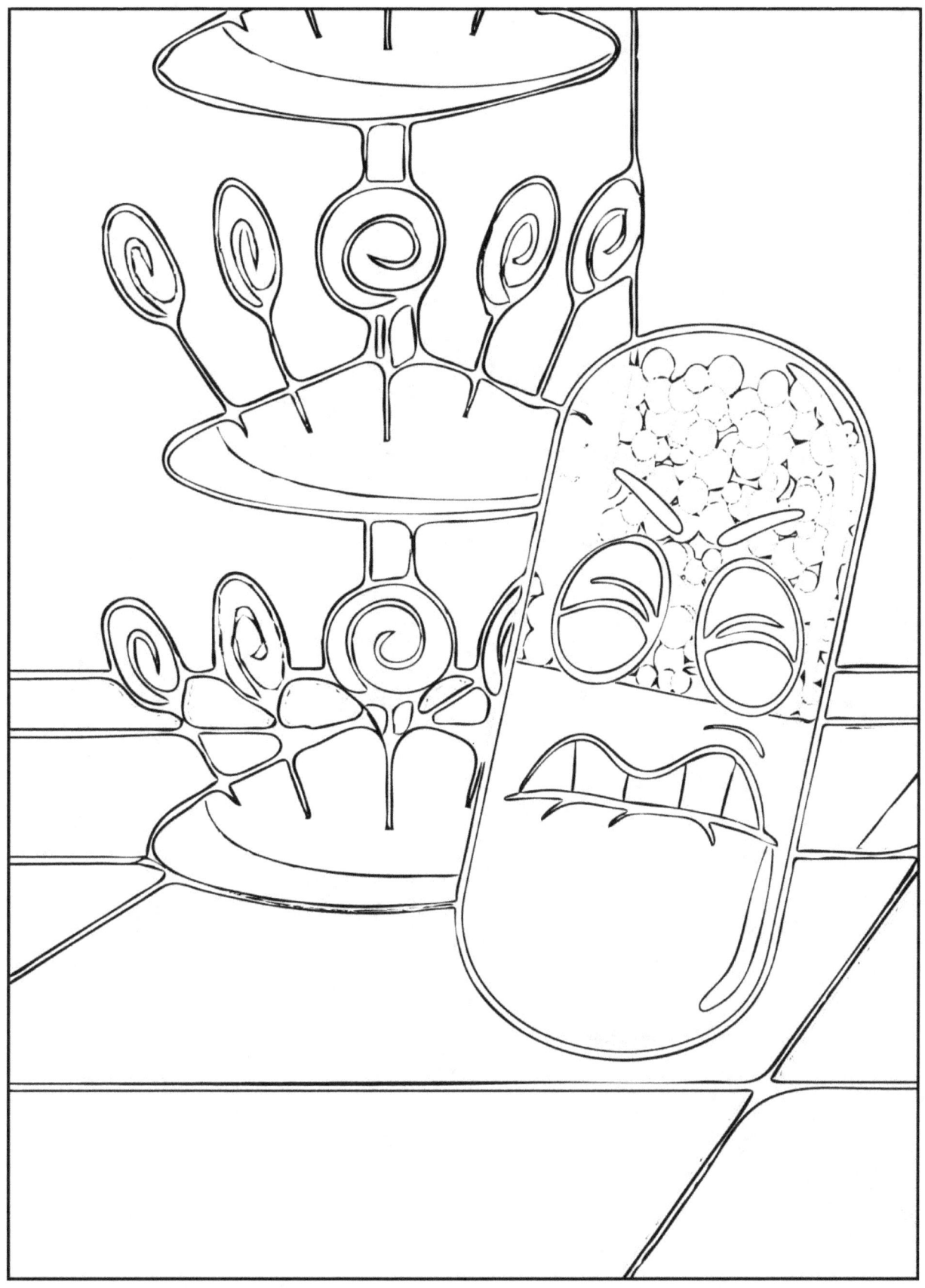

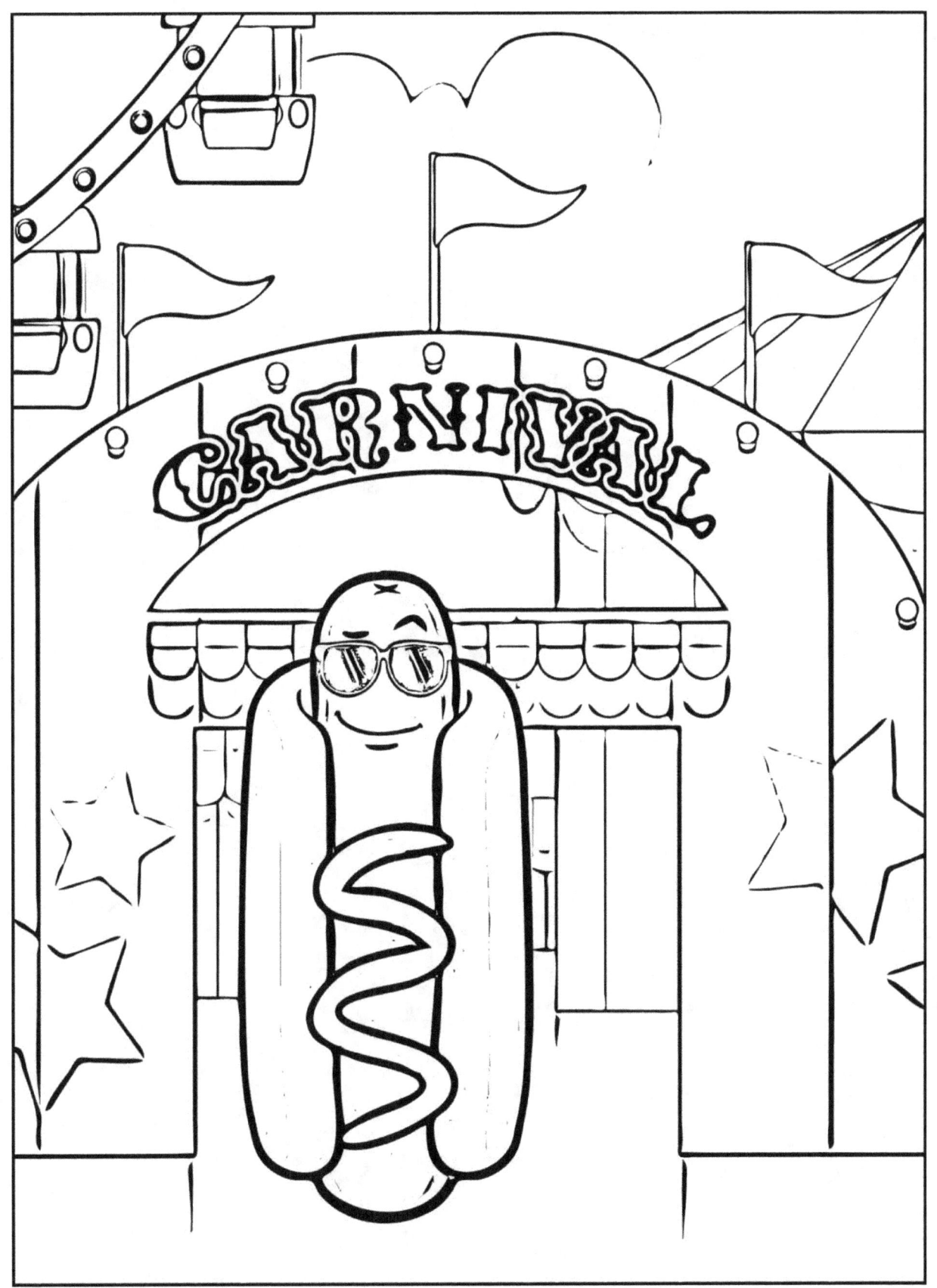

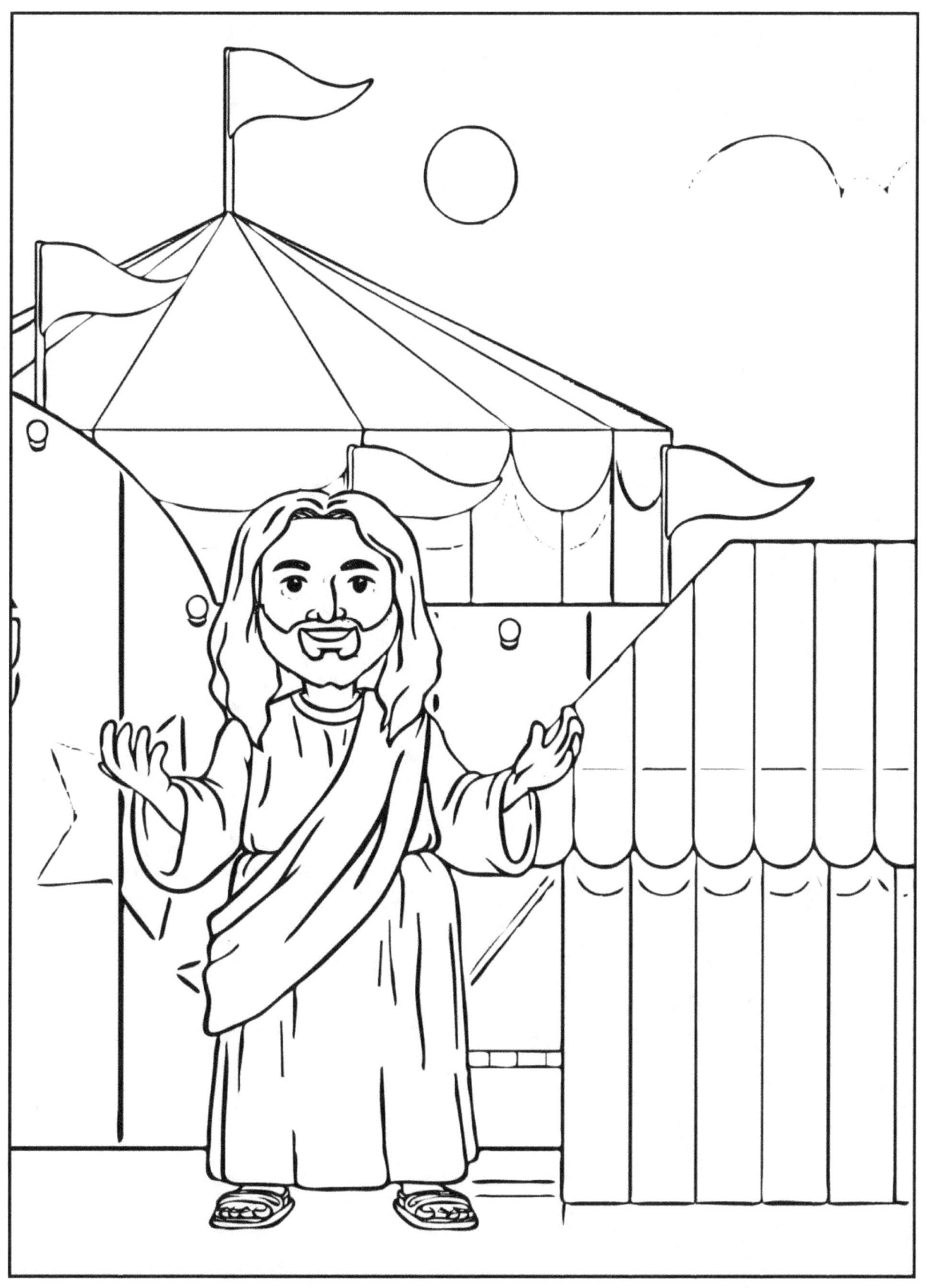

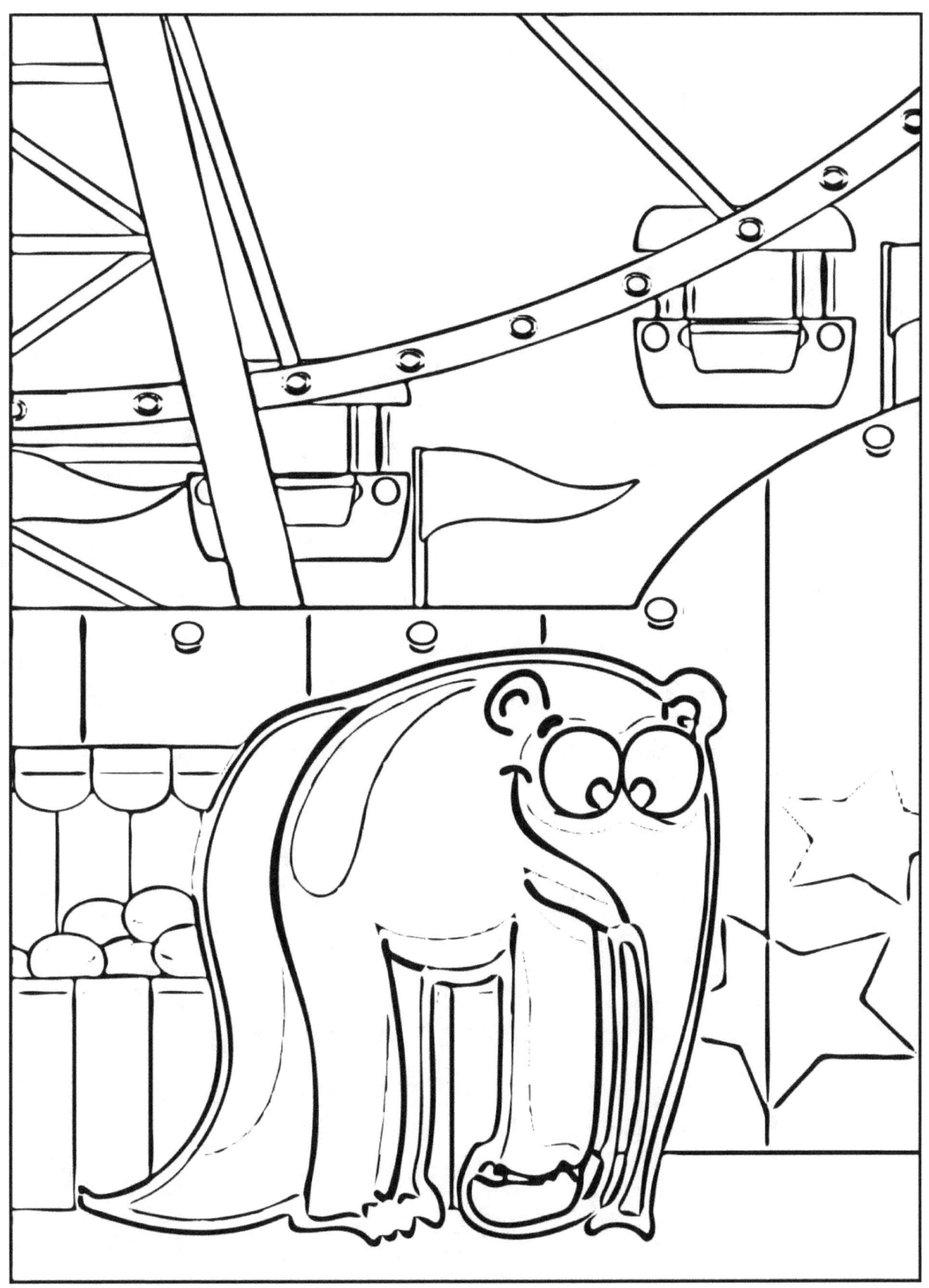

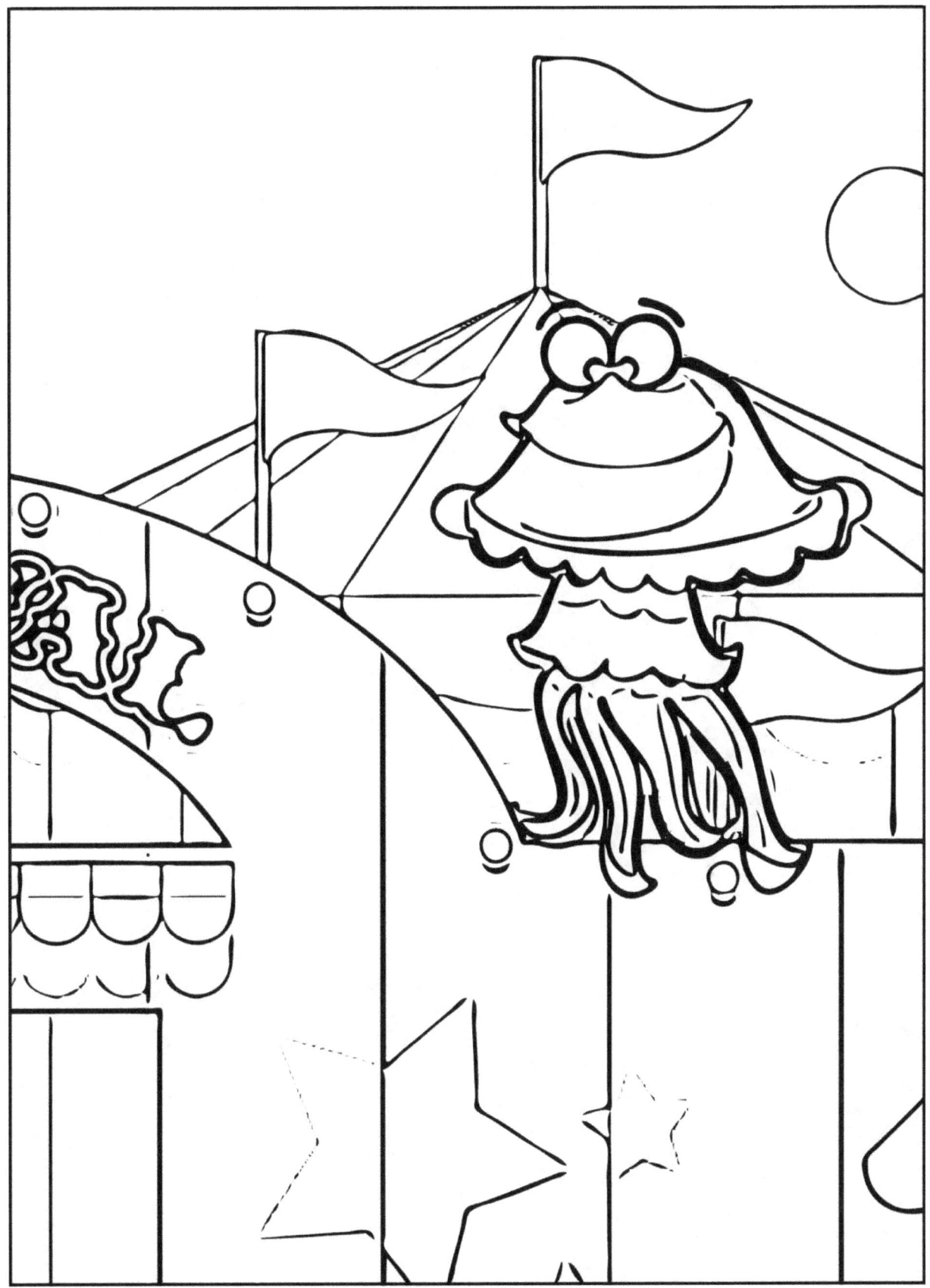

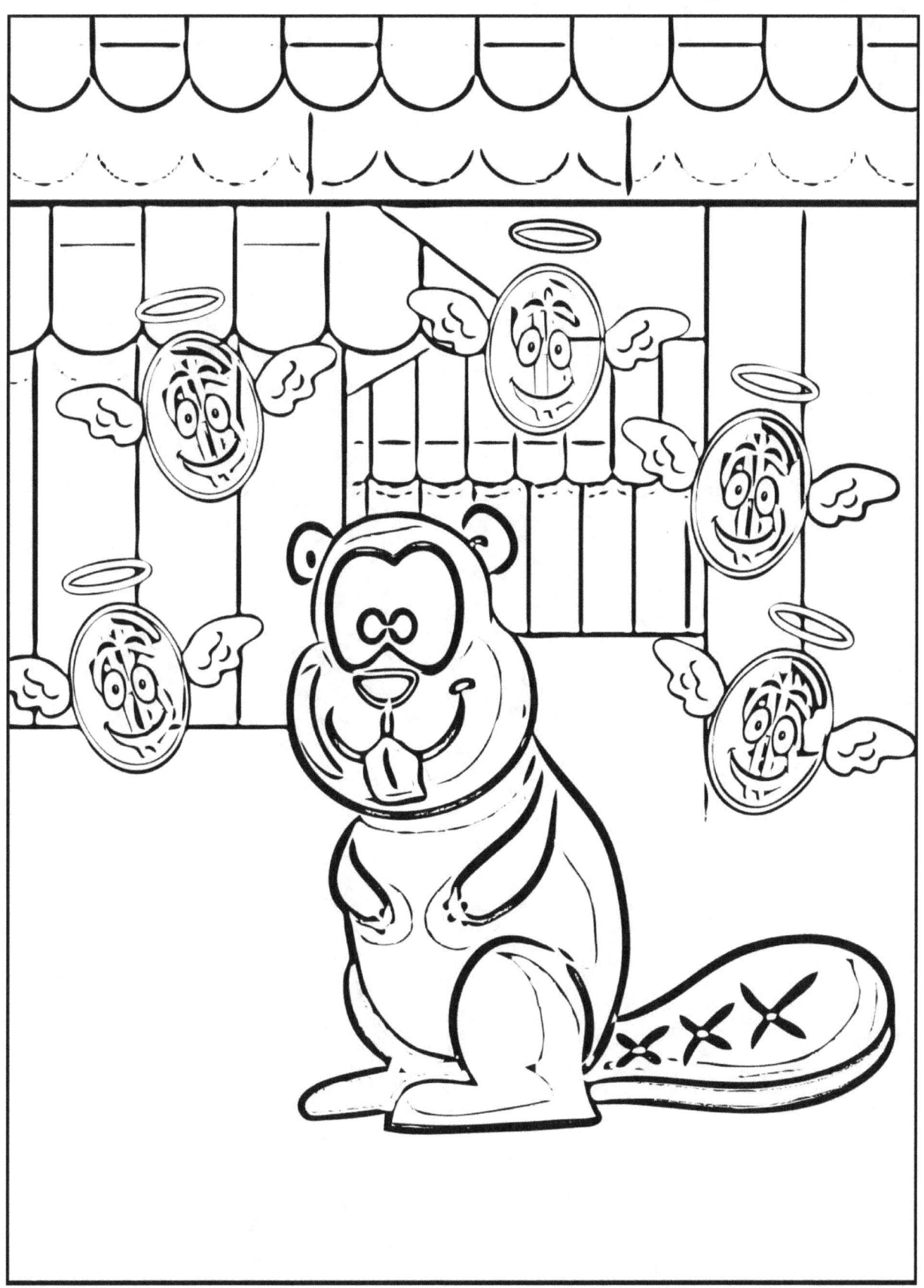

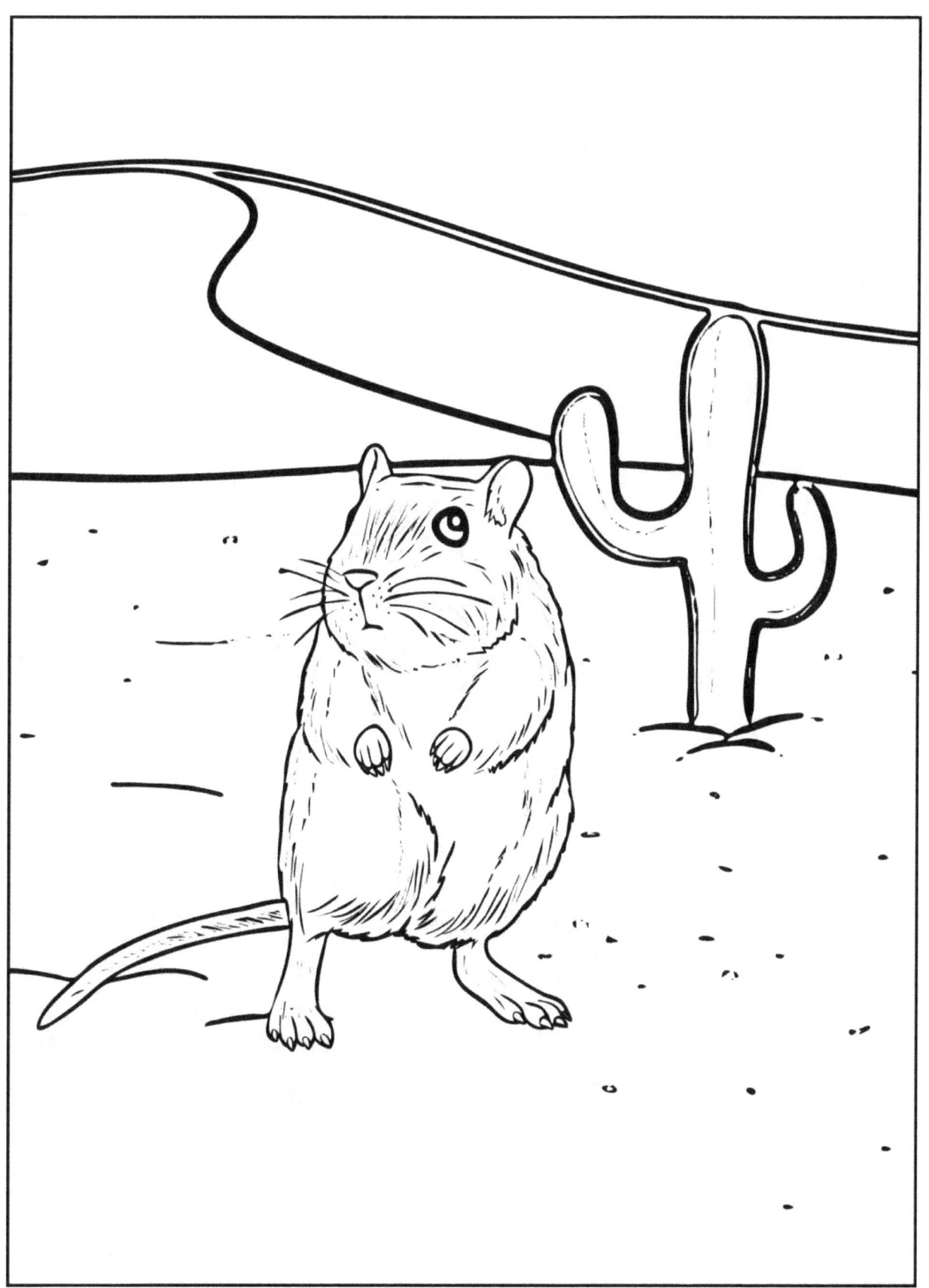

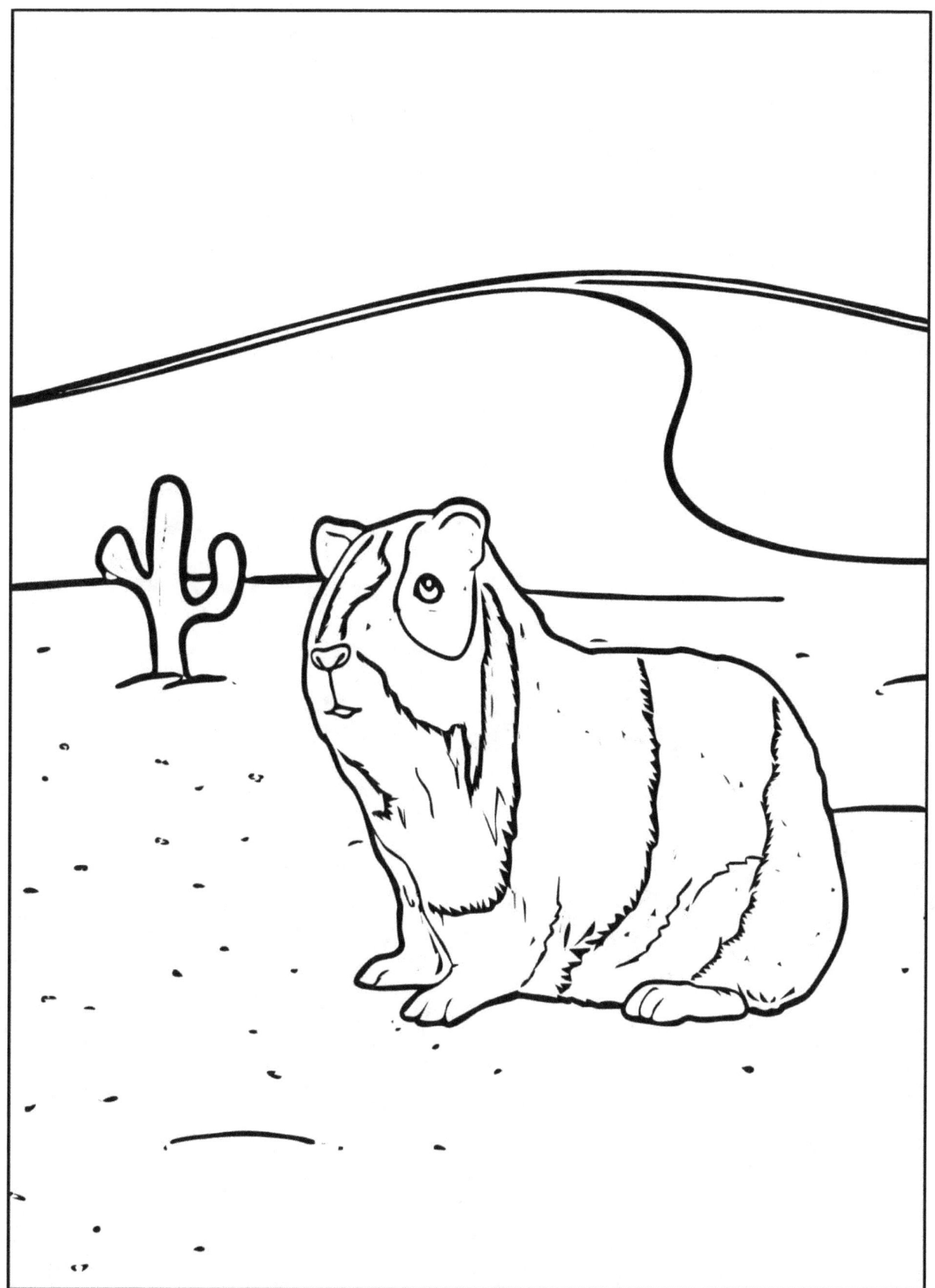

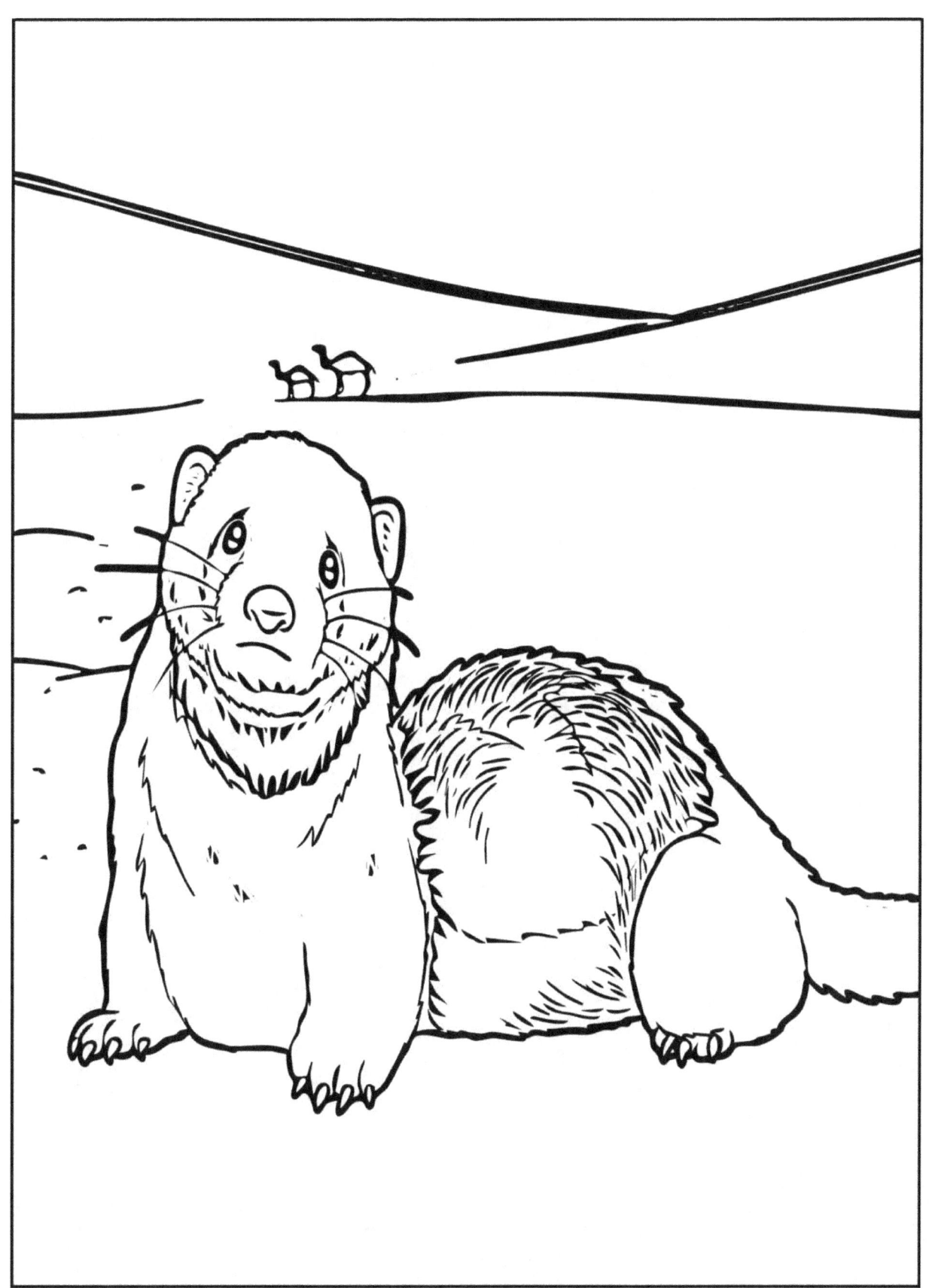

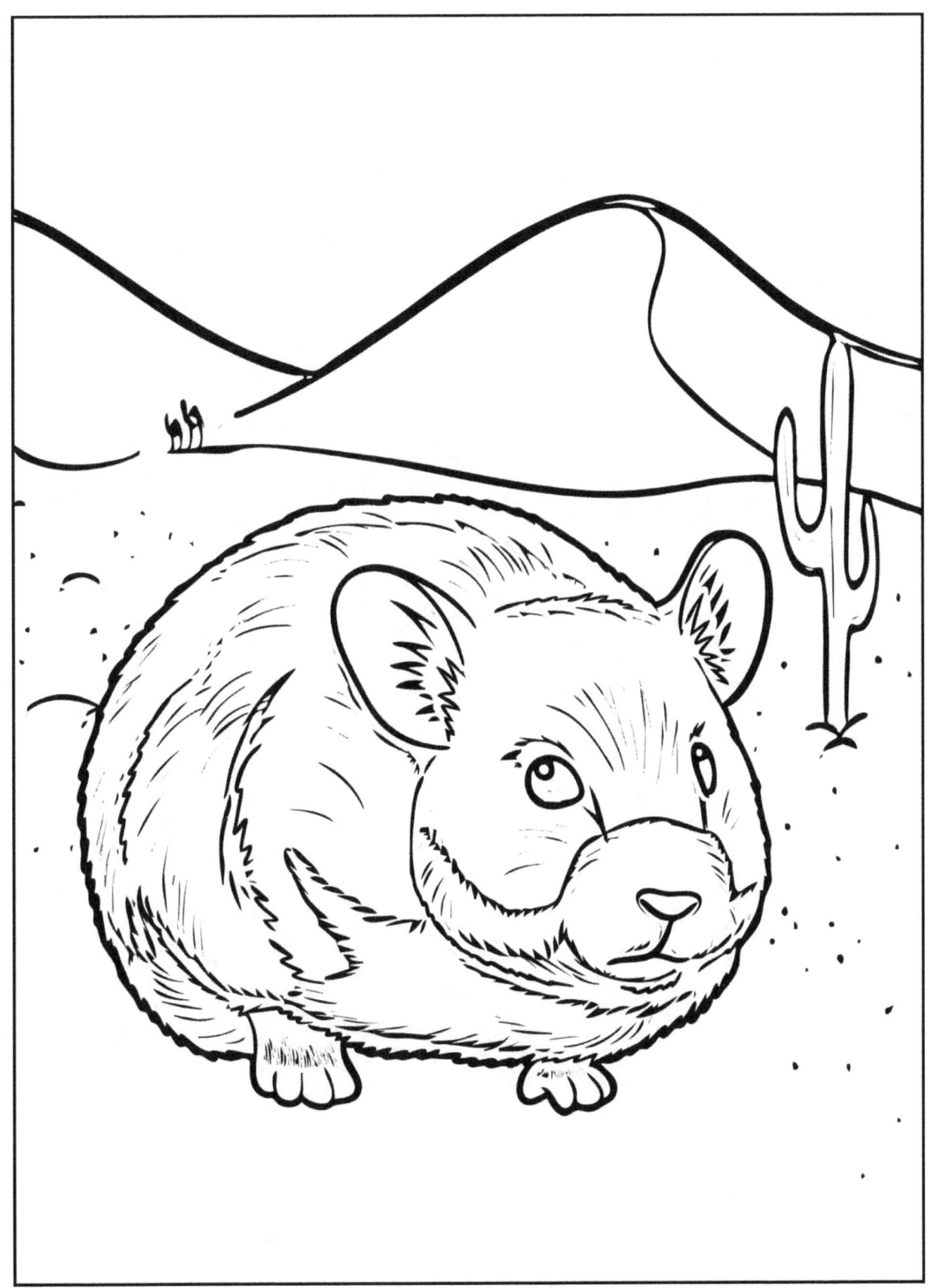

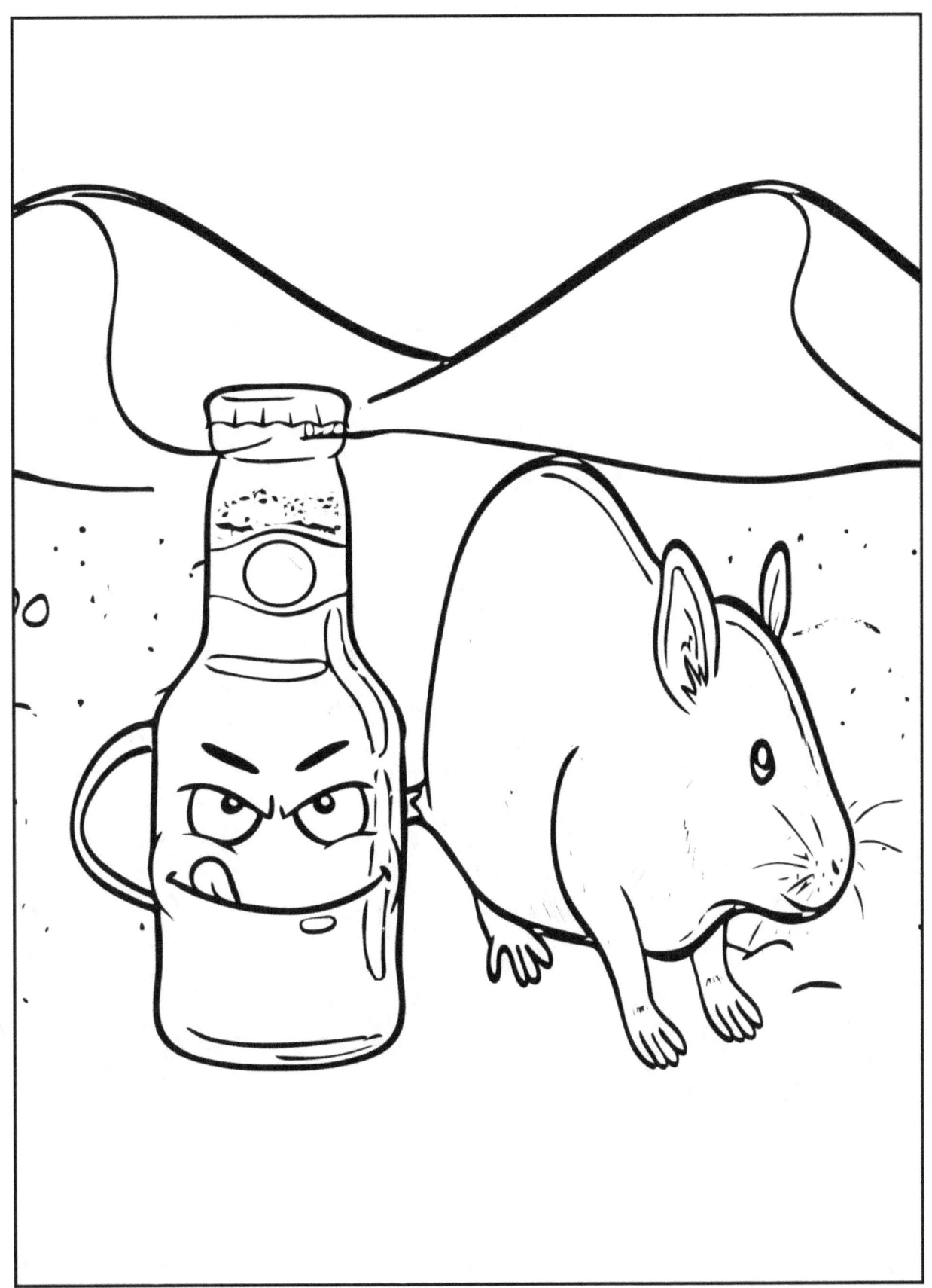

KOOKY COLORING BOOK

For All Ages

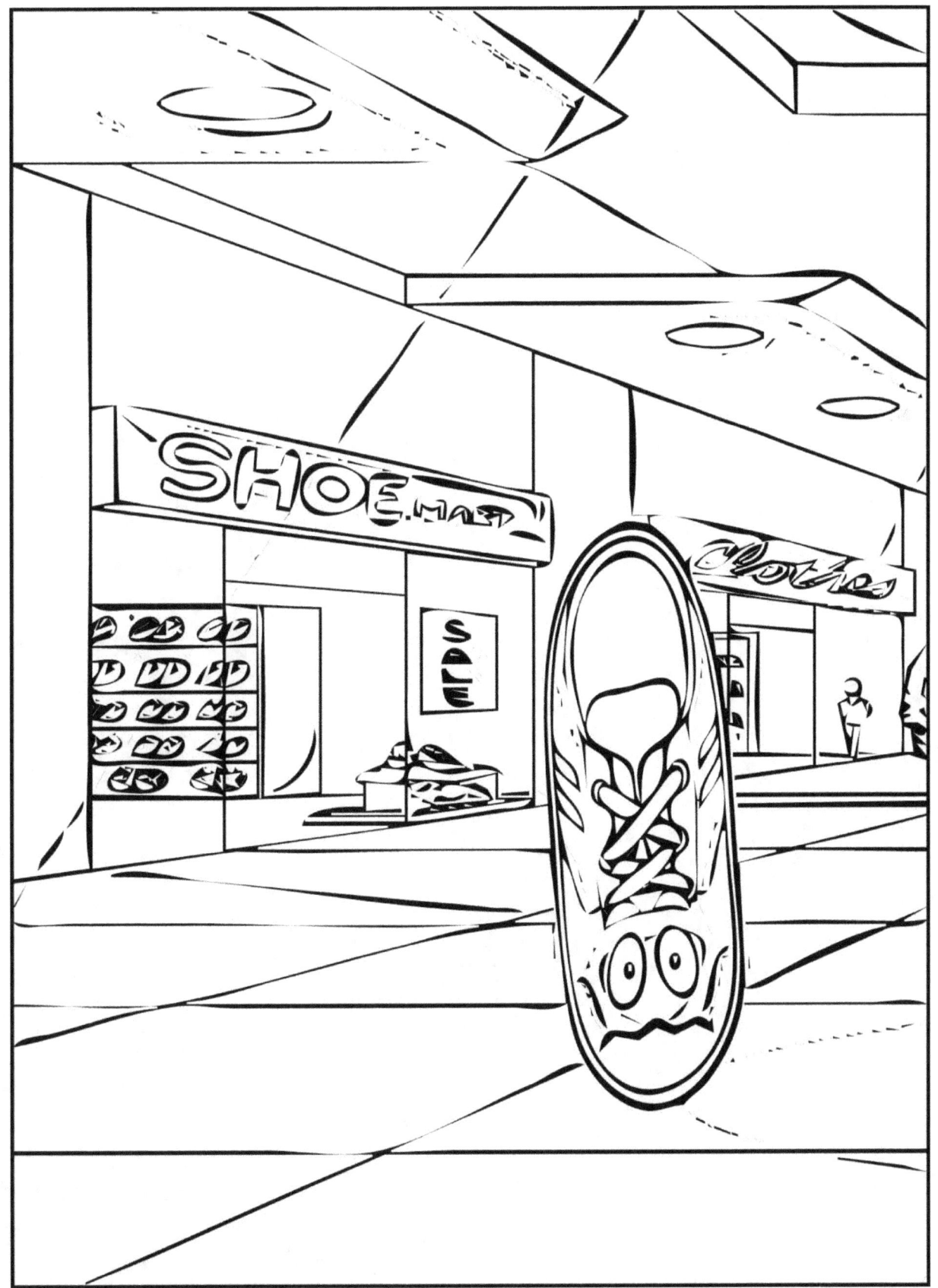

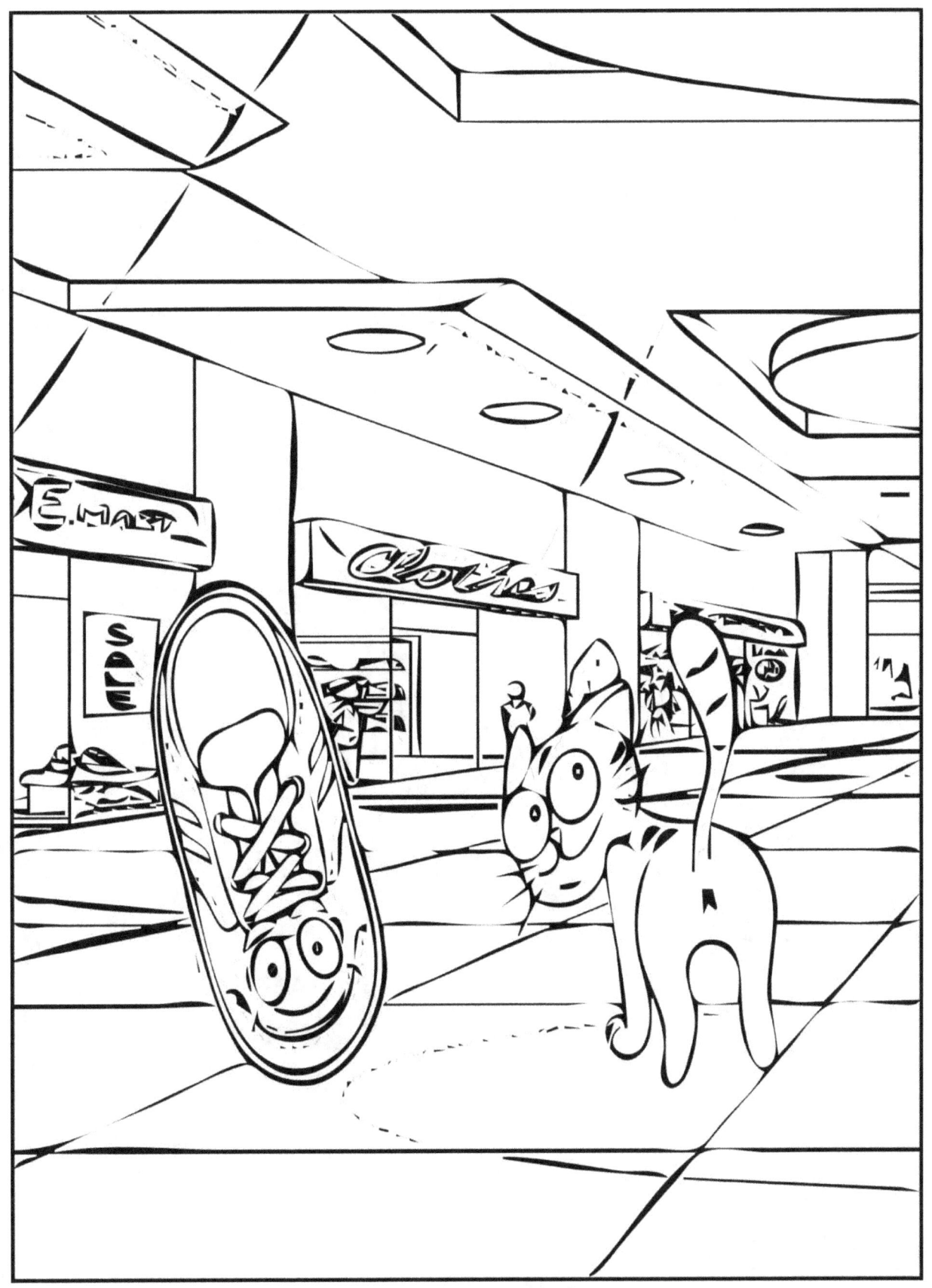

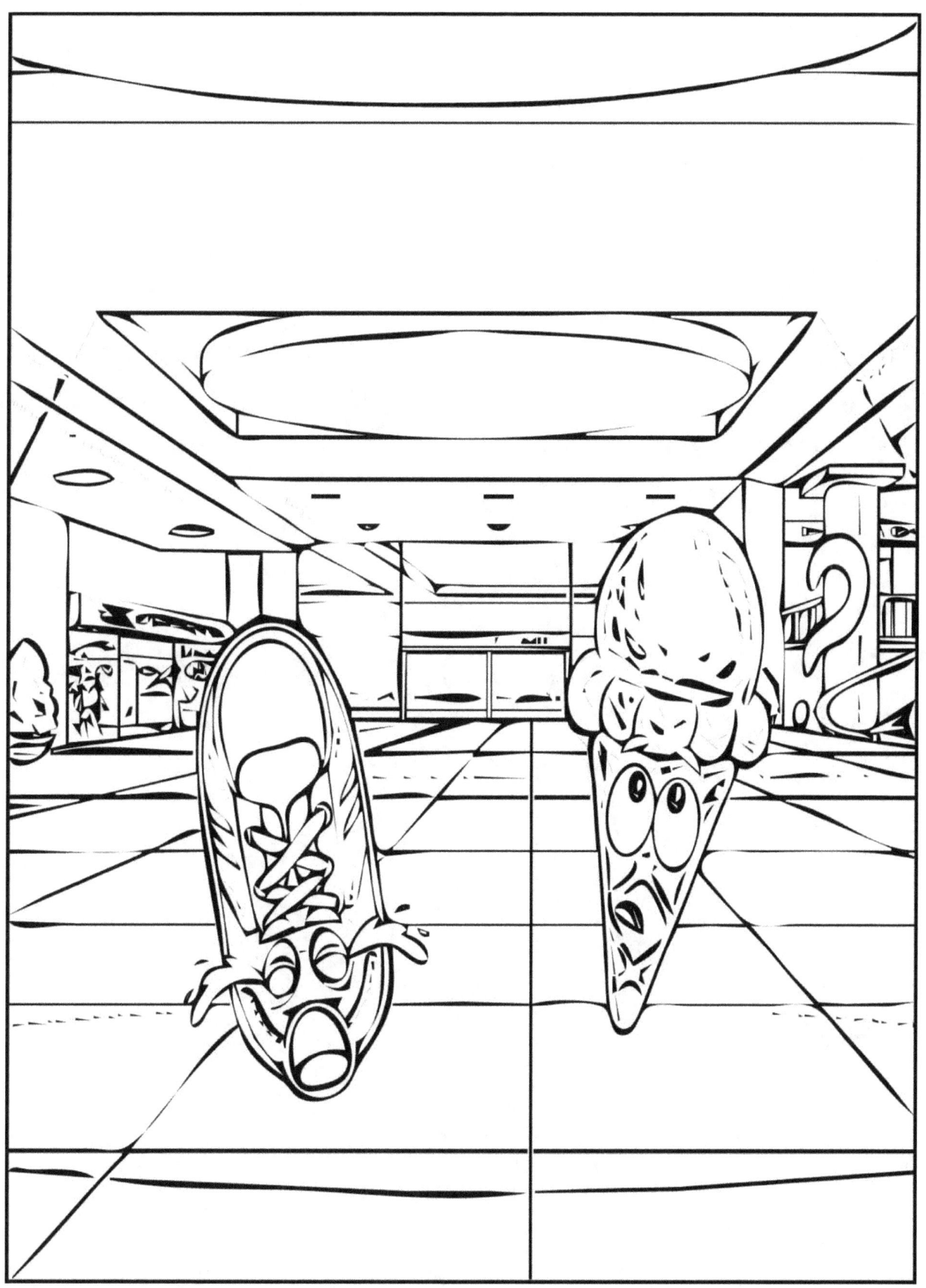

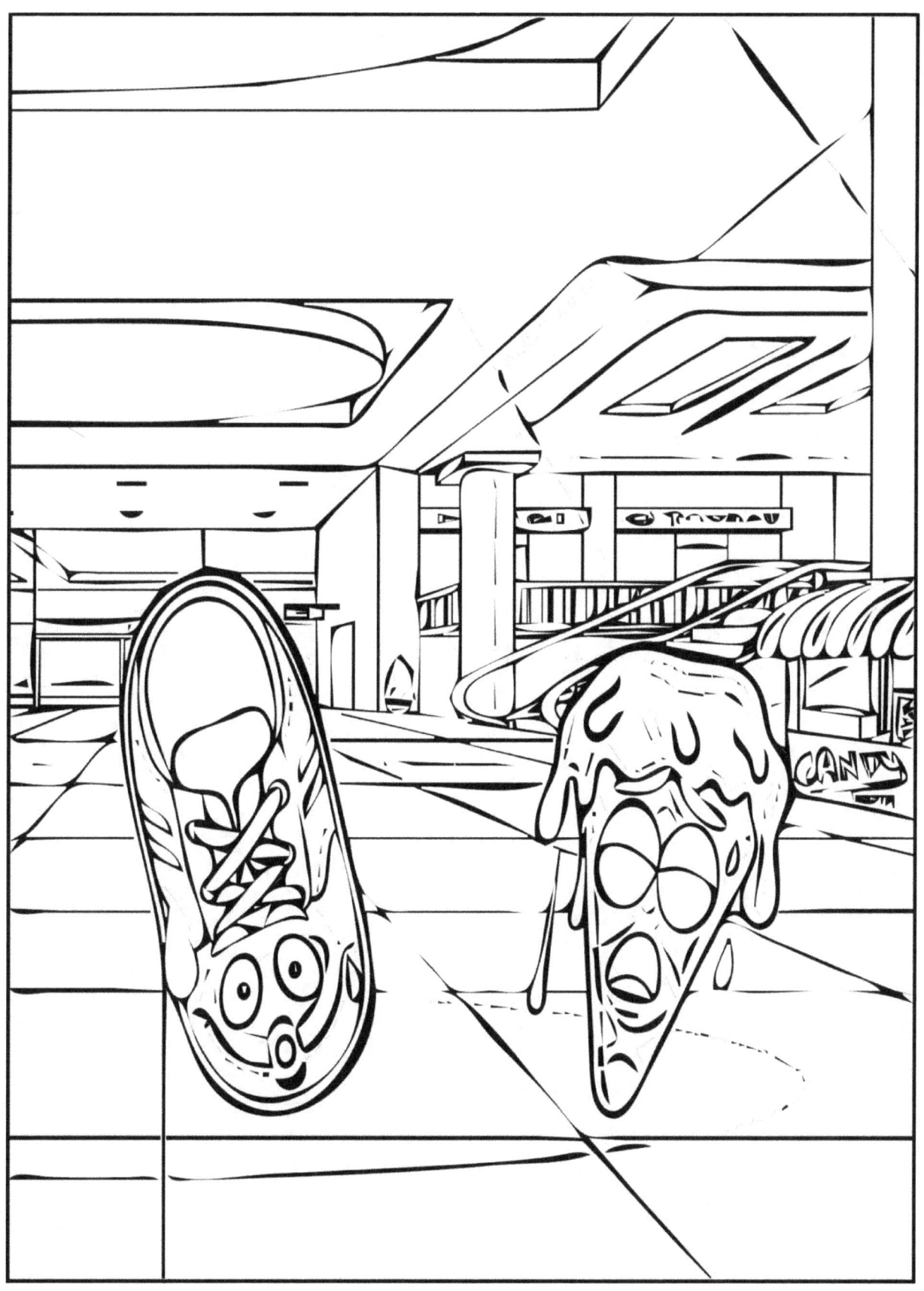

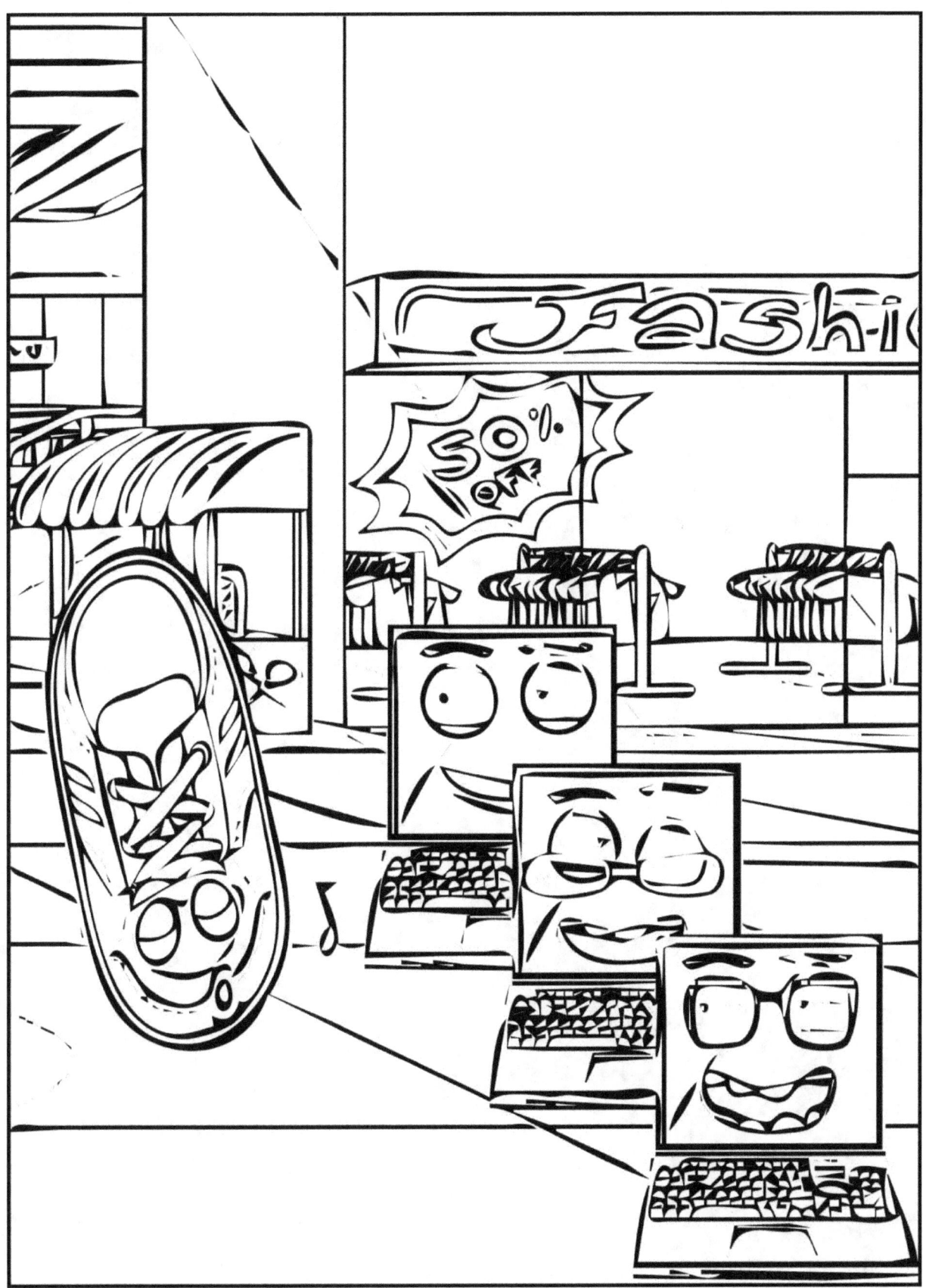

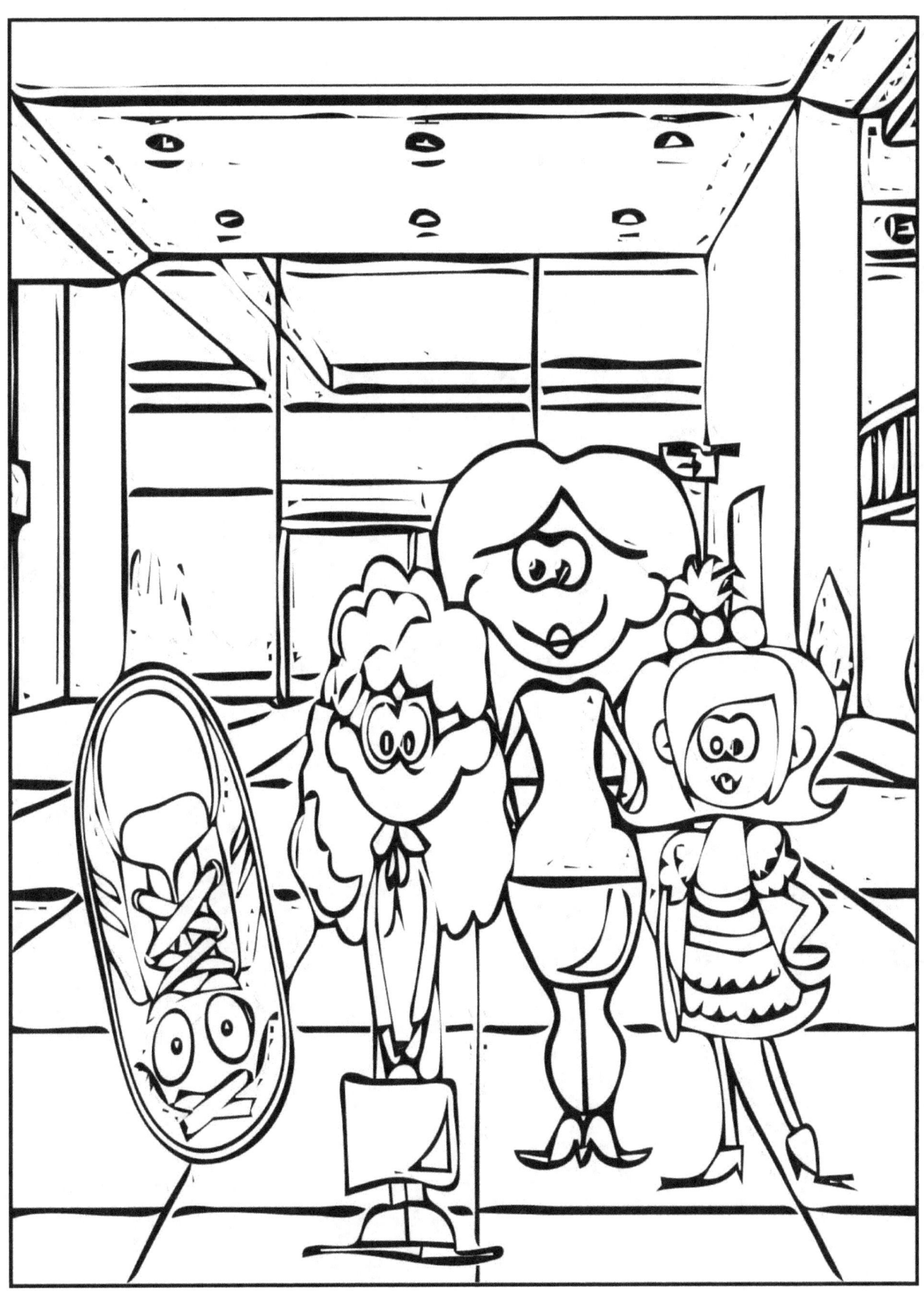

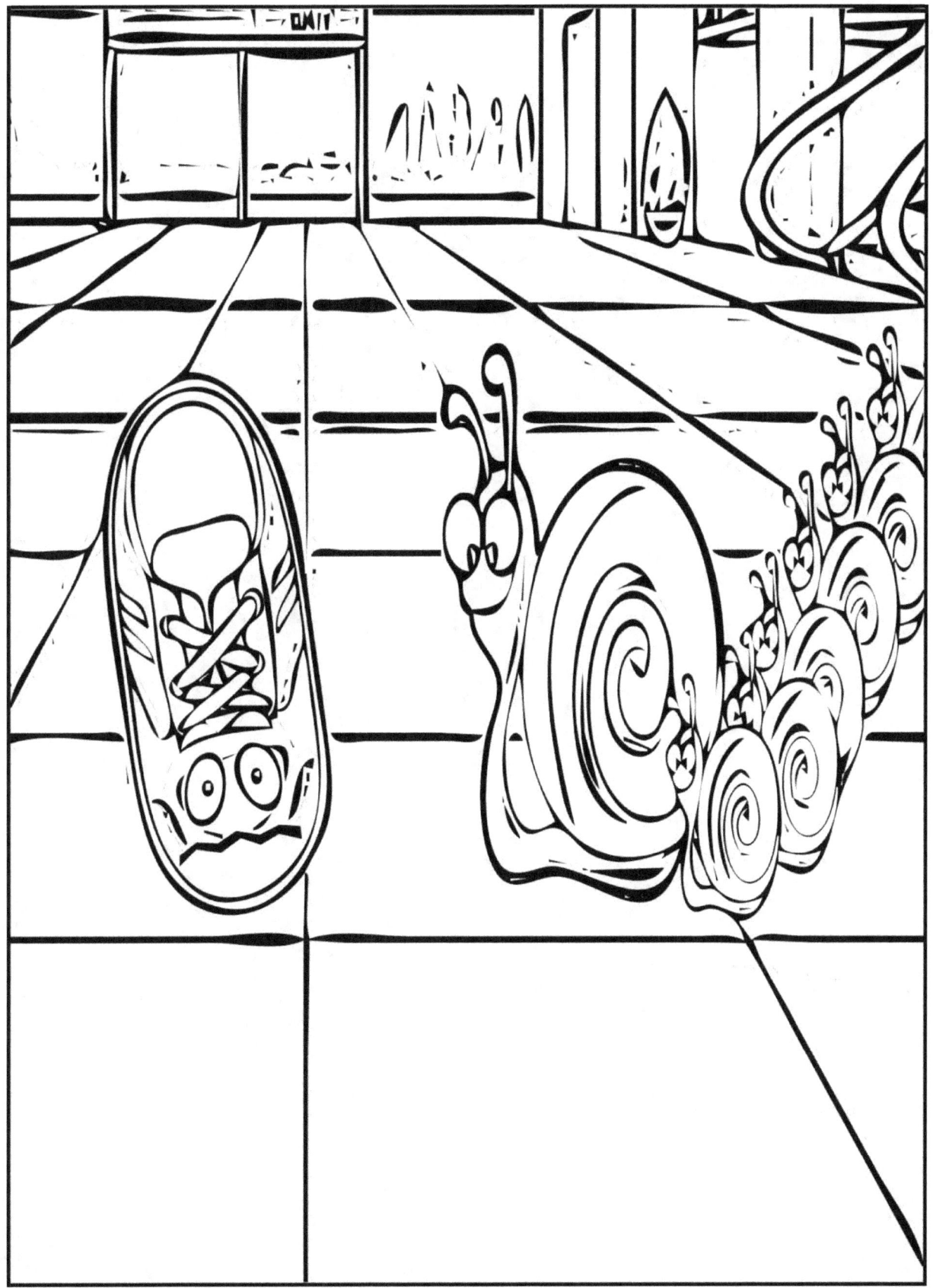

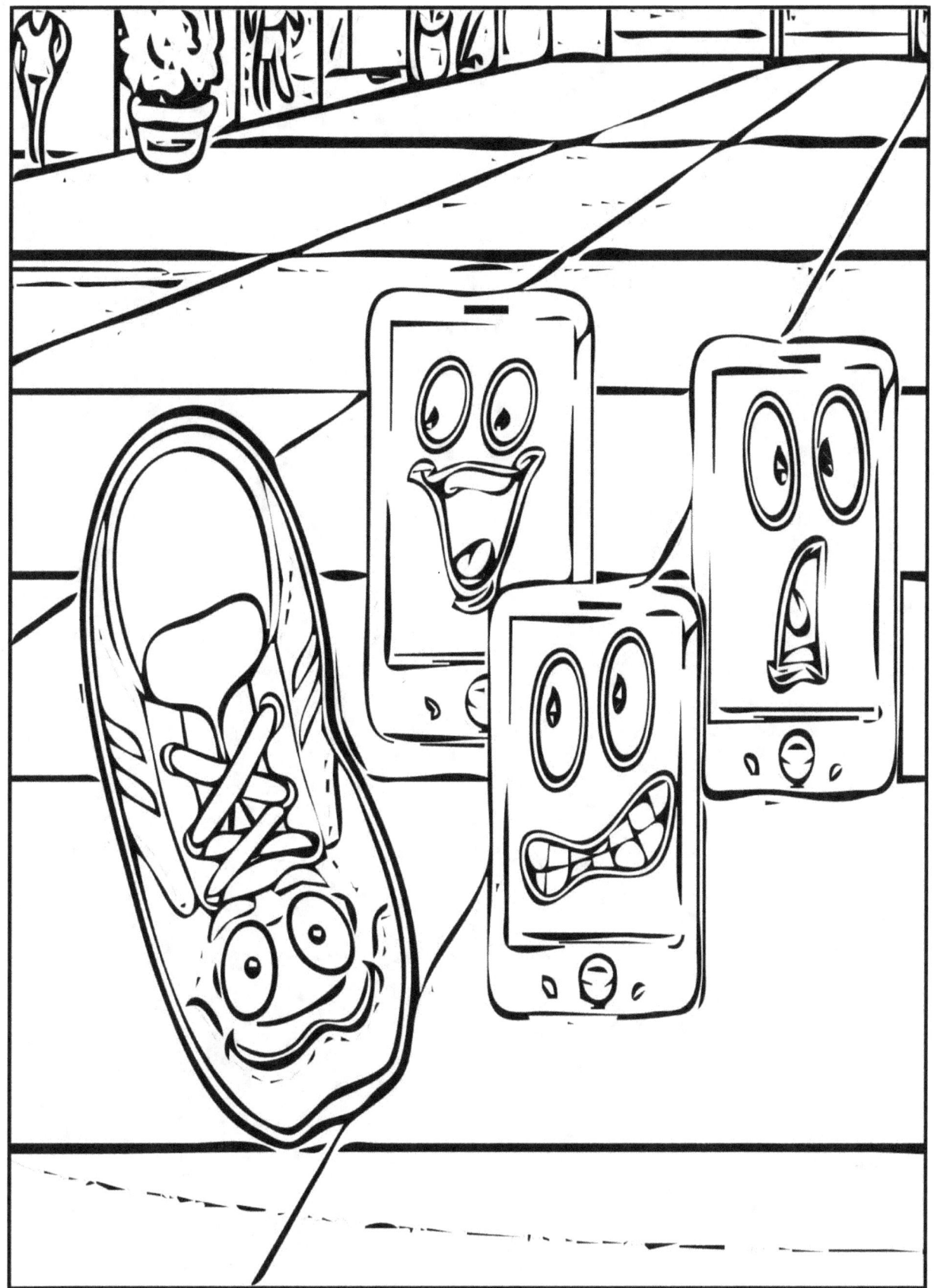

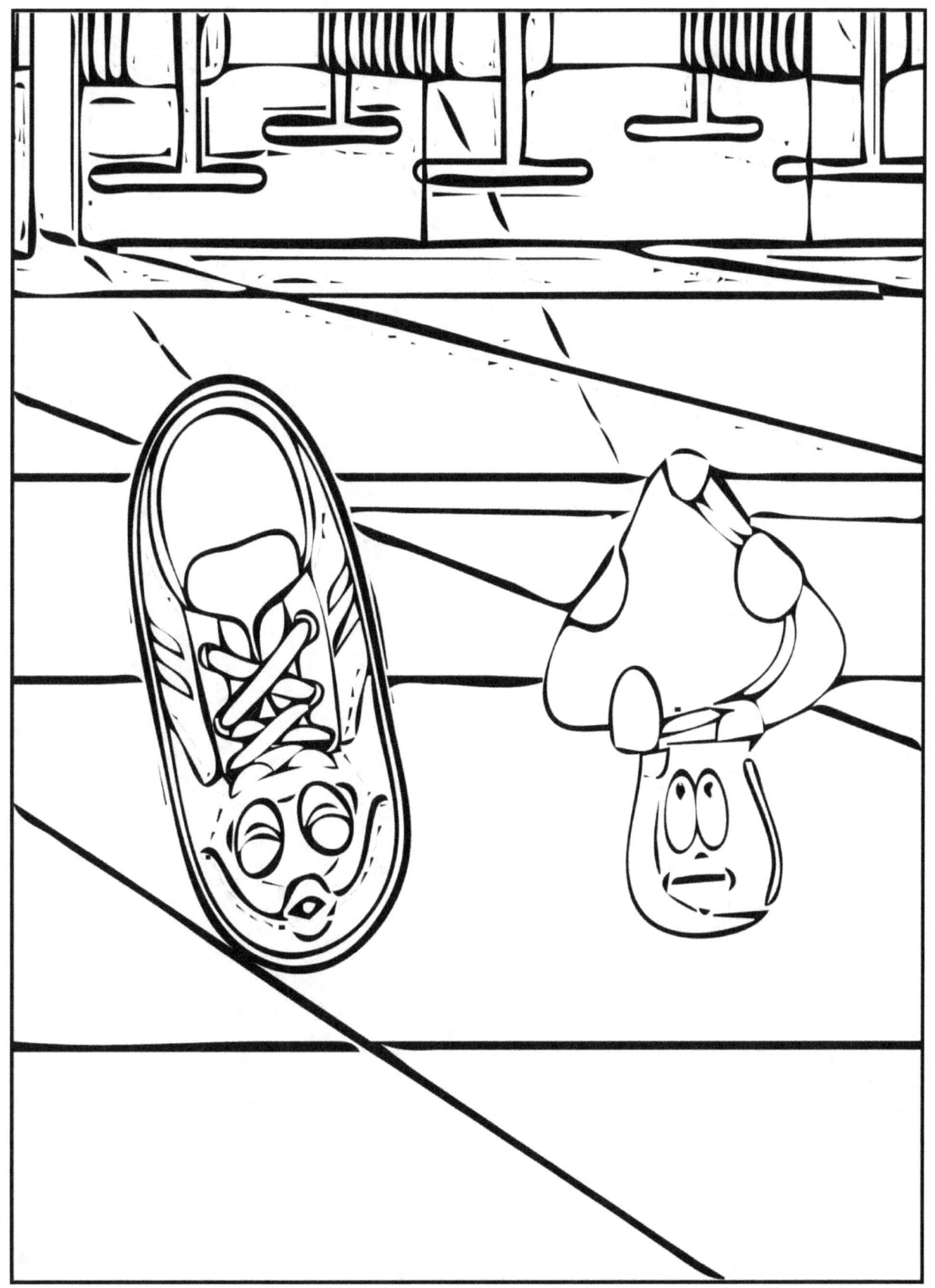

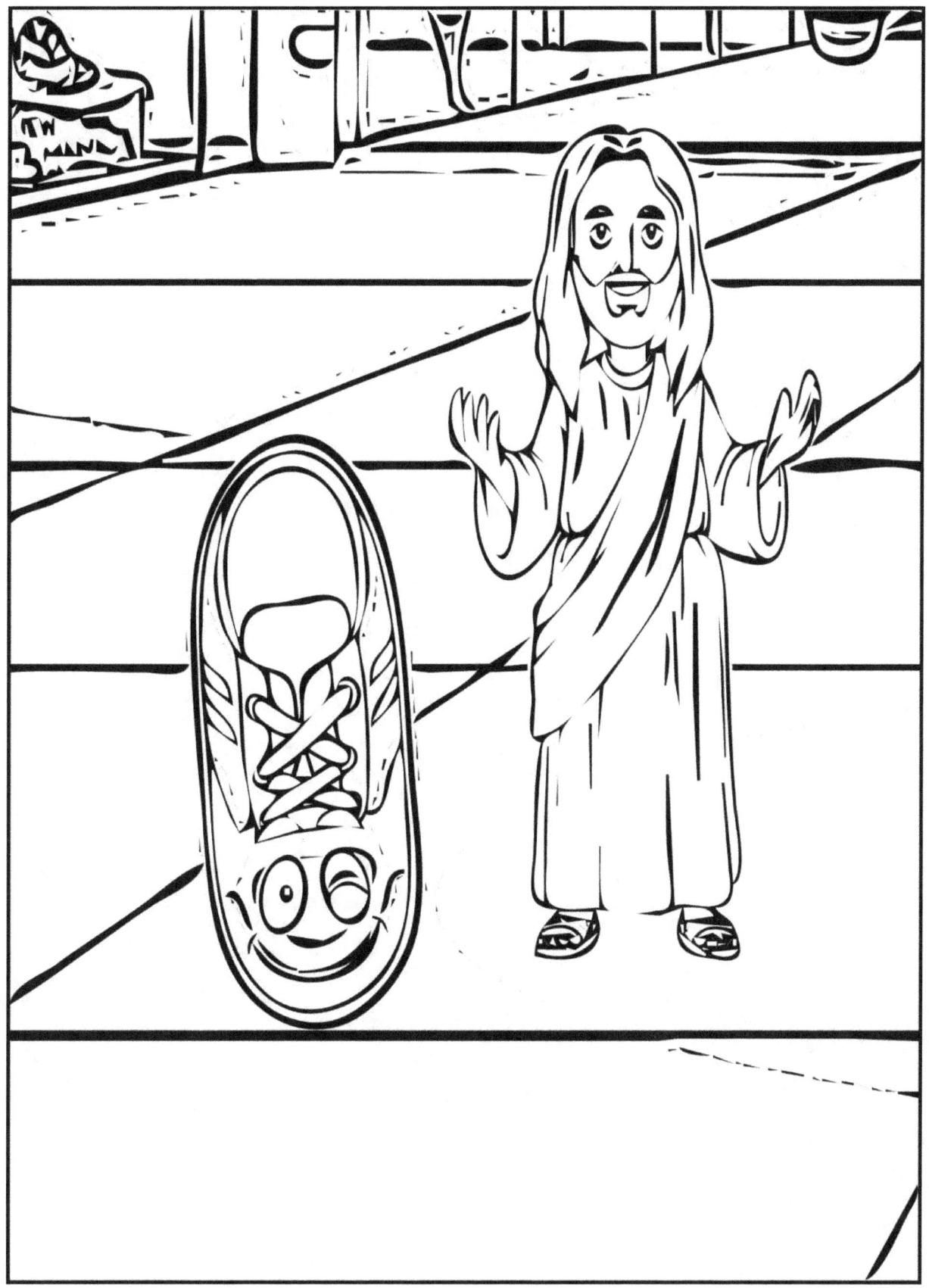

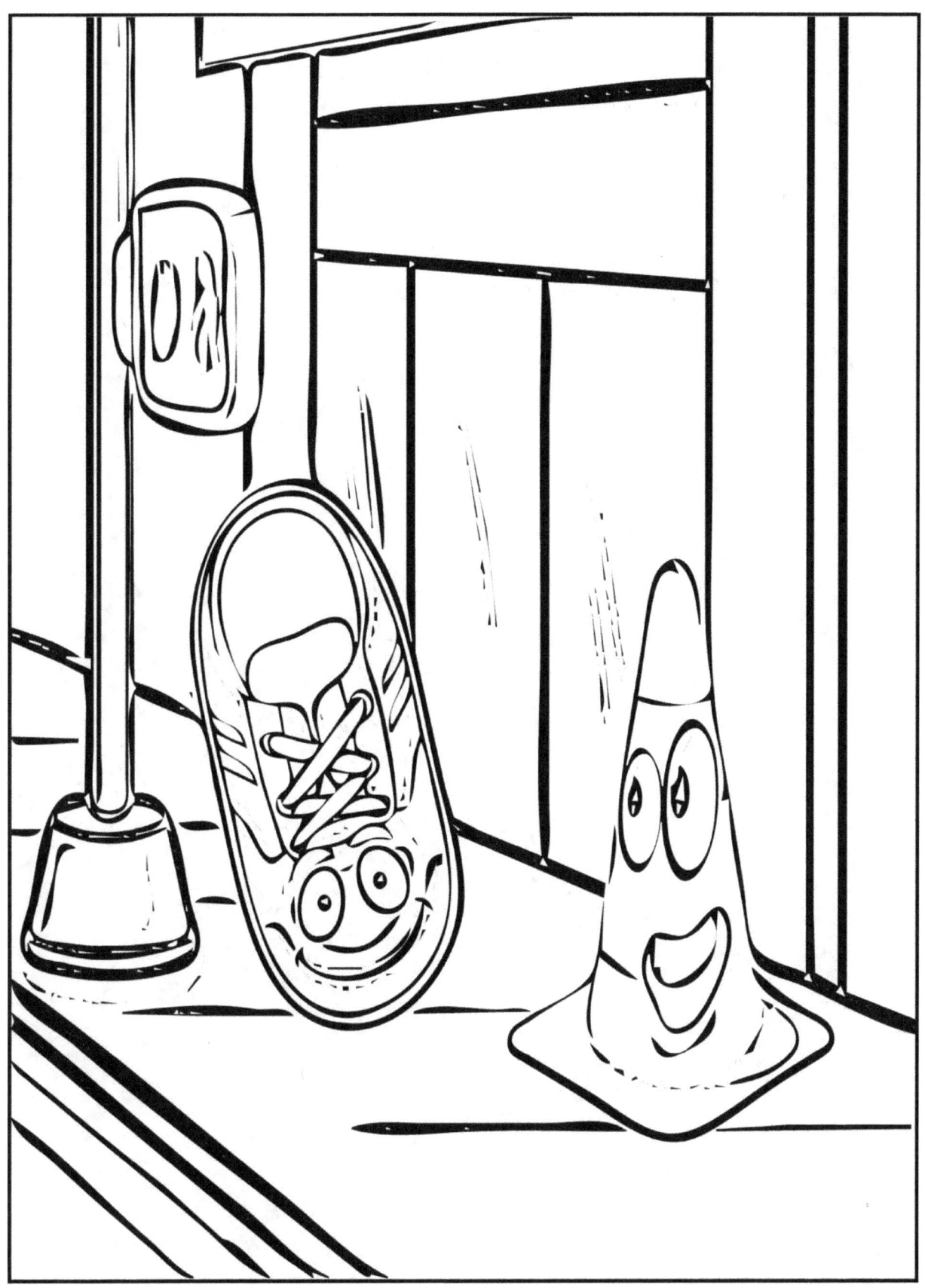

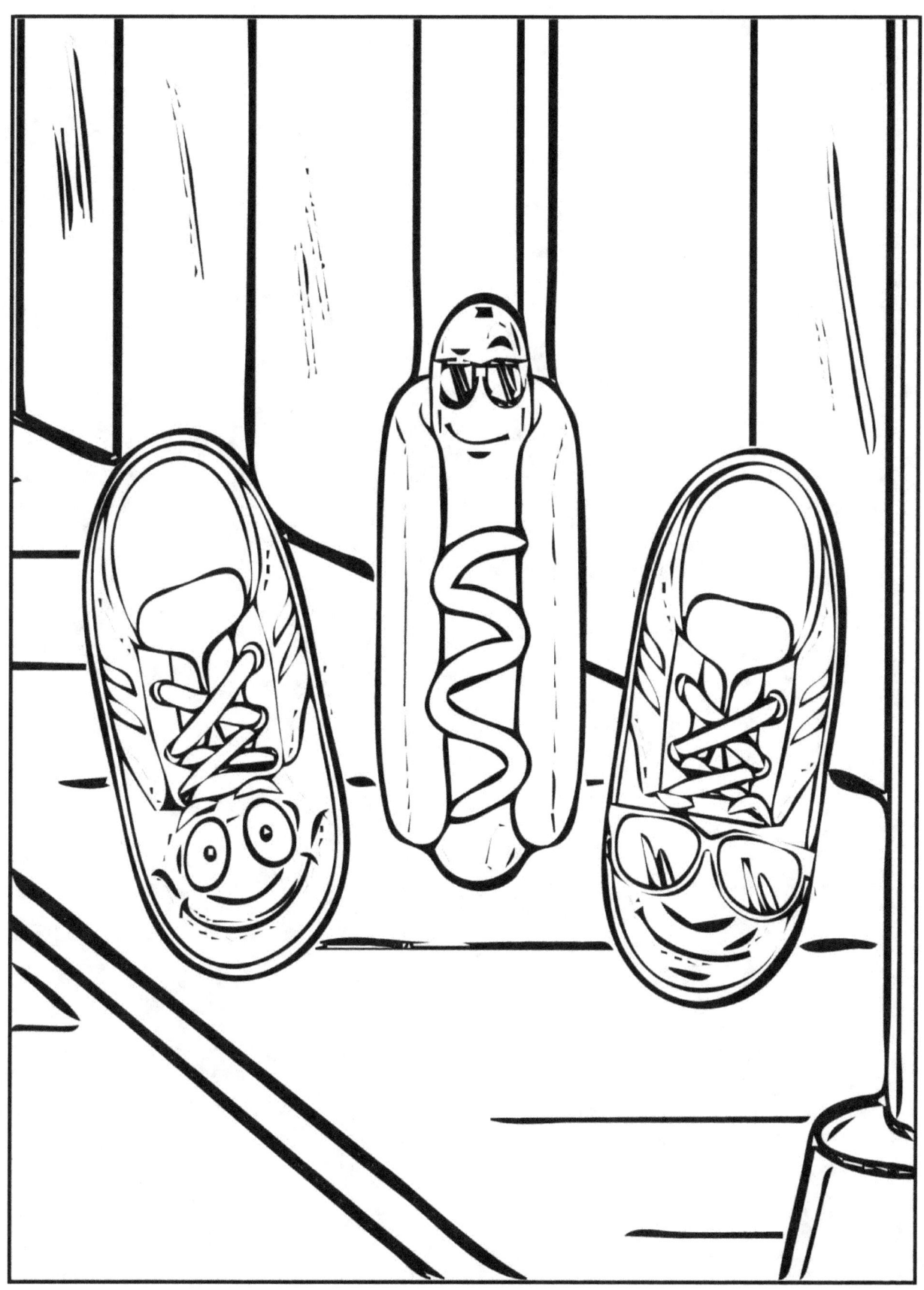

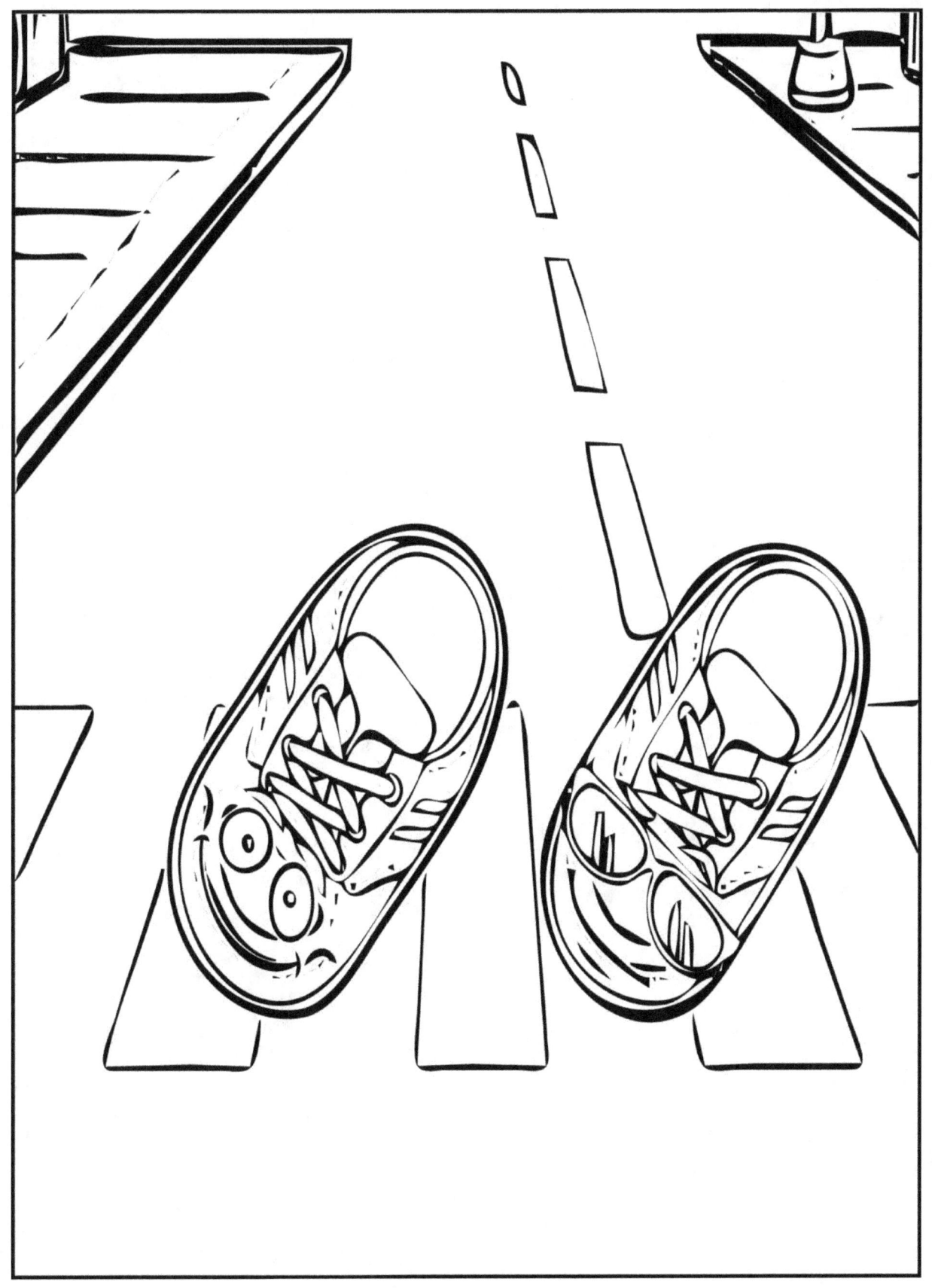

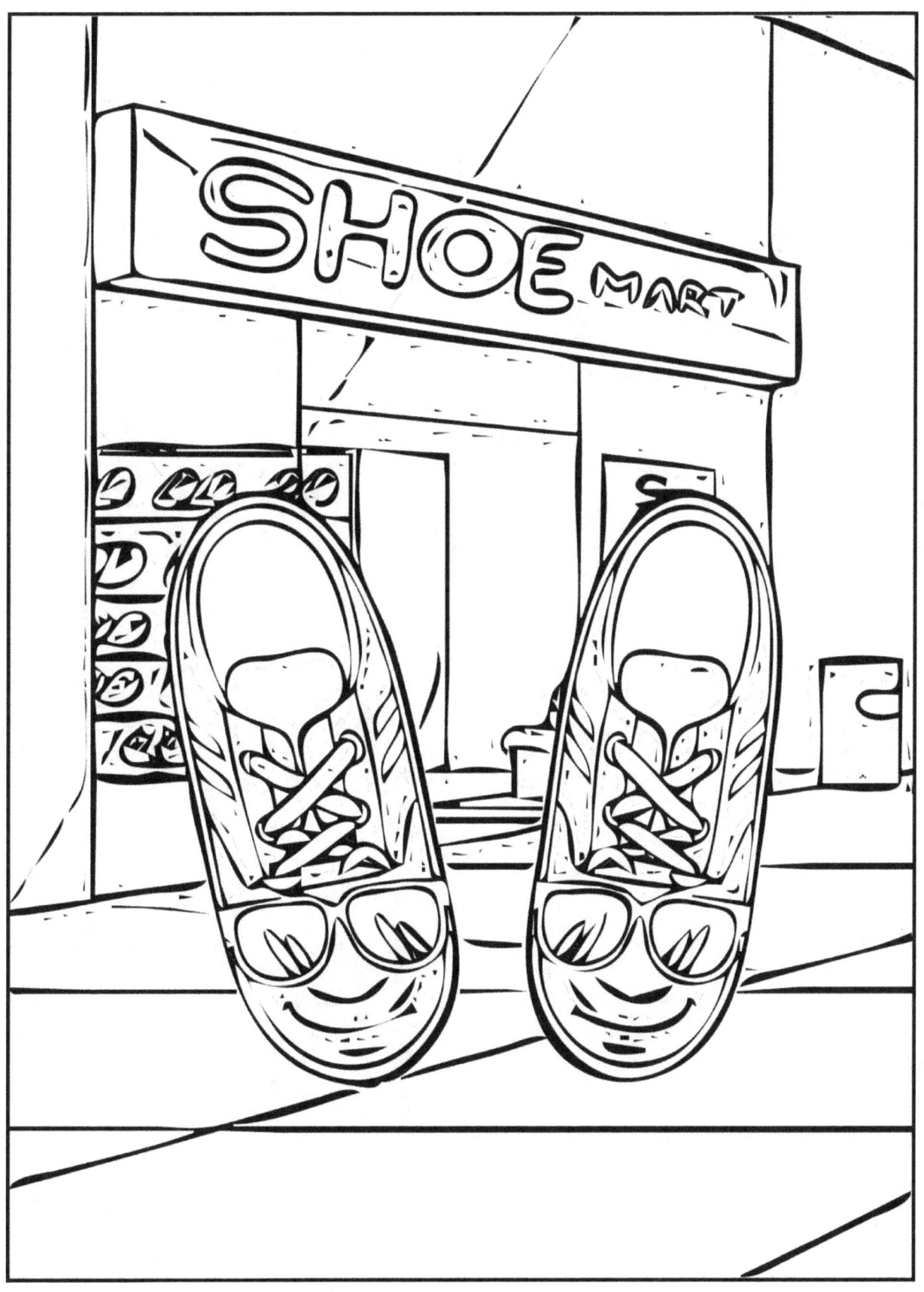

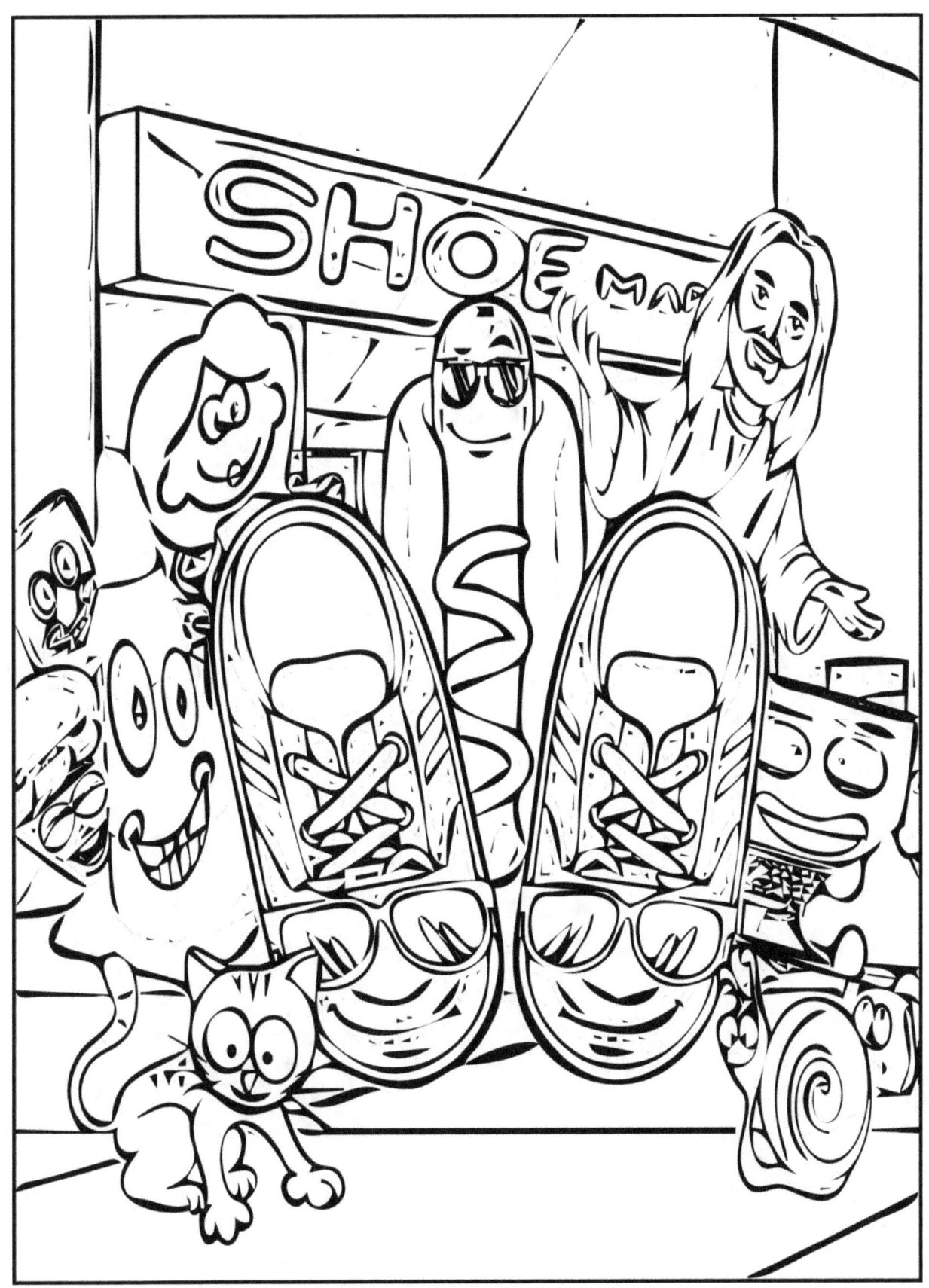

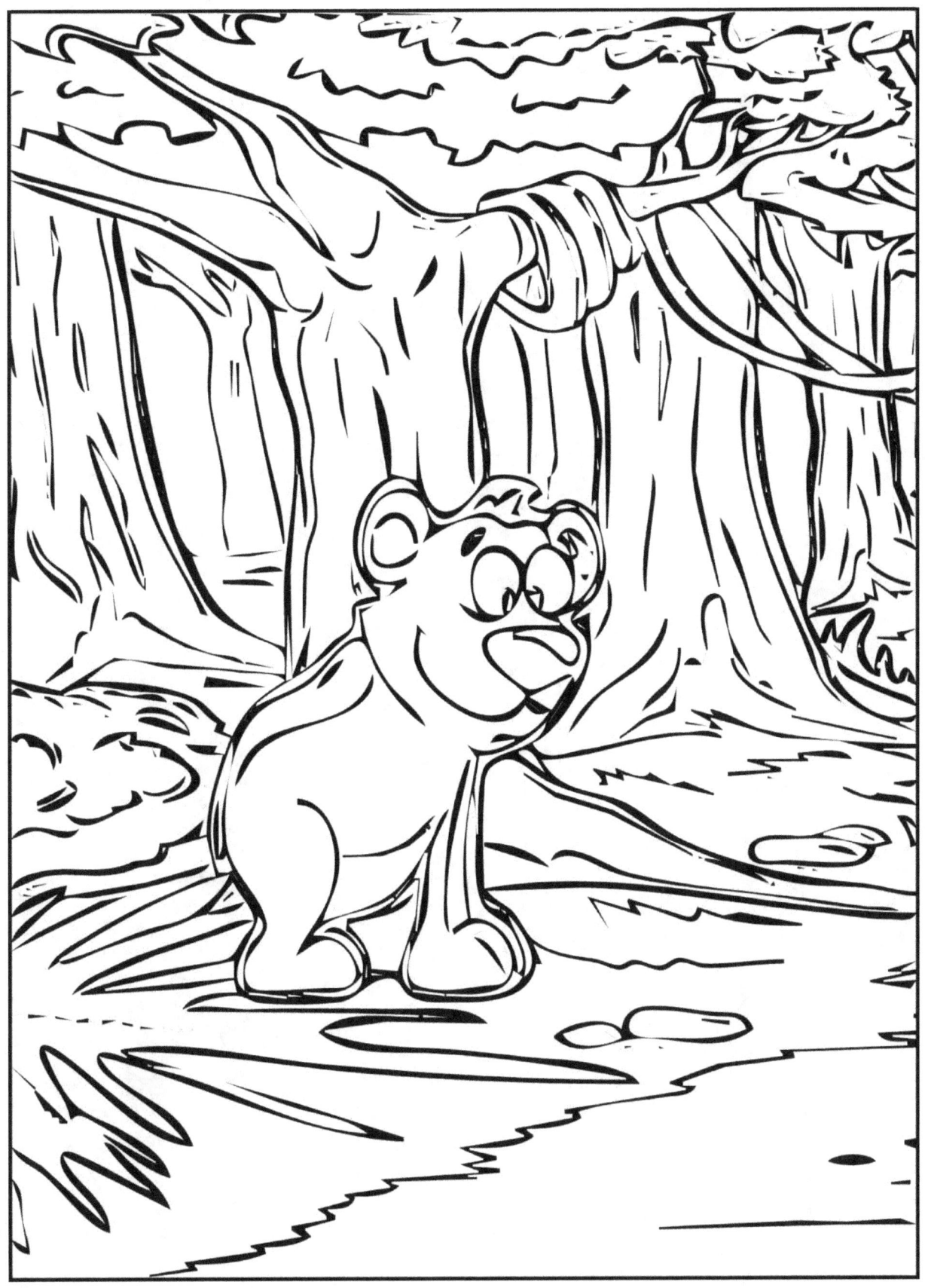

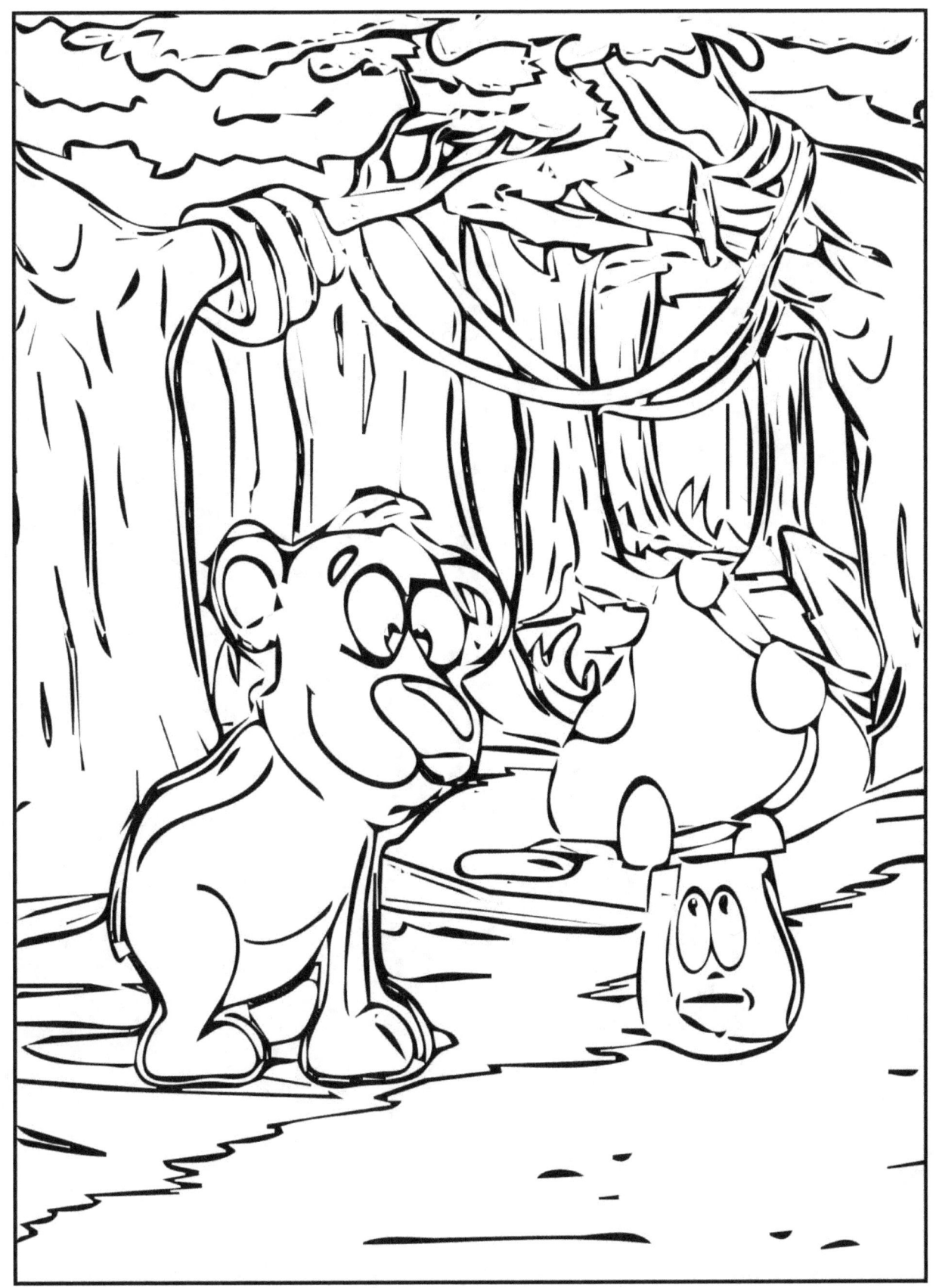

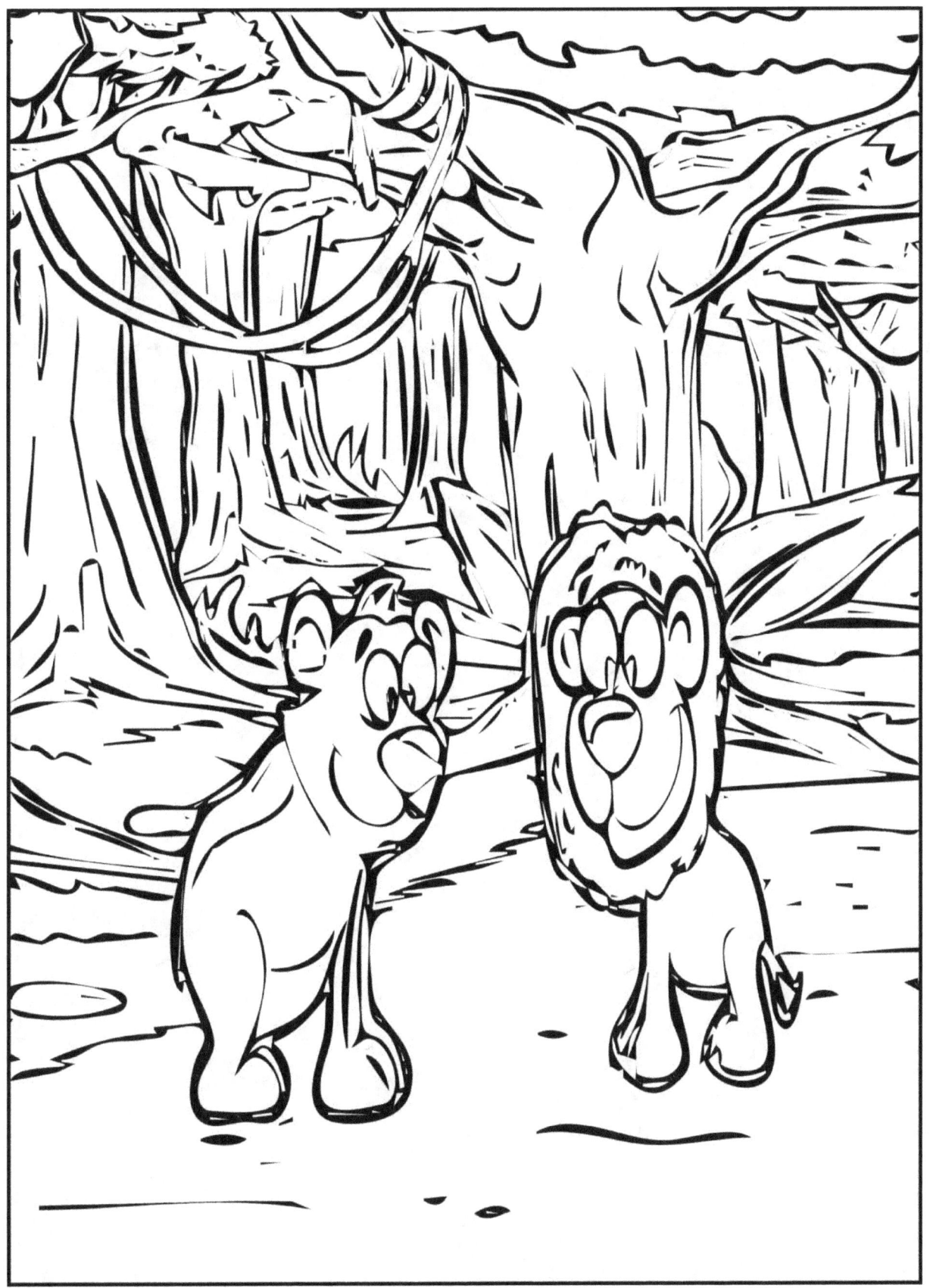

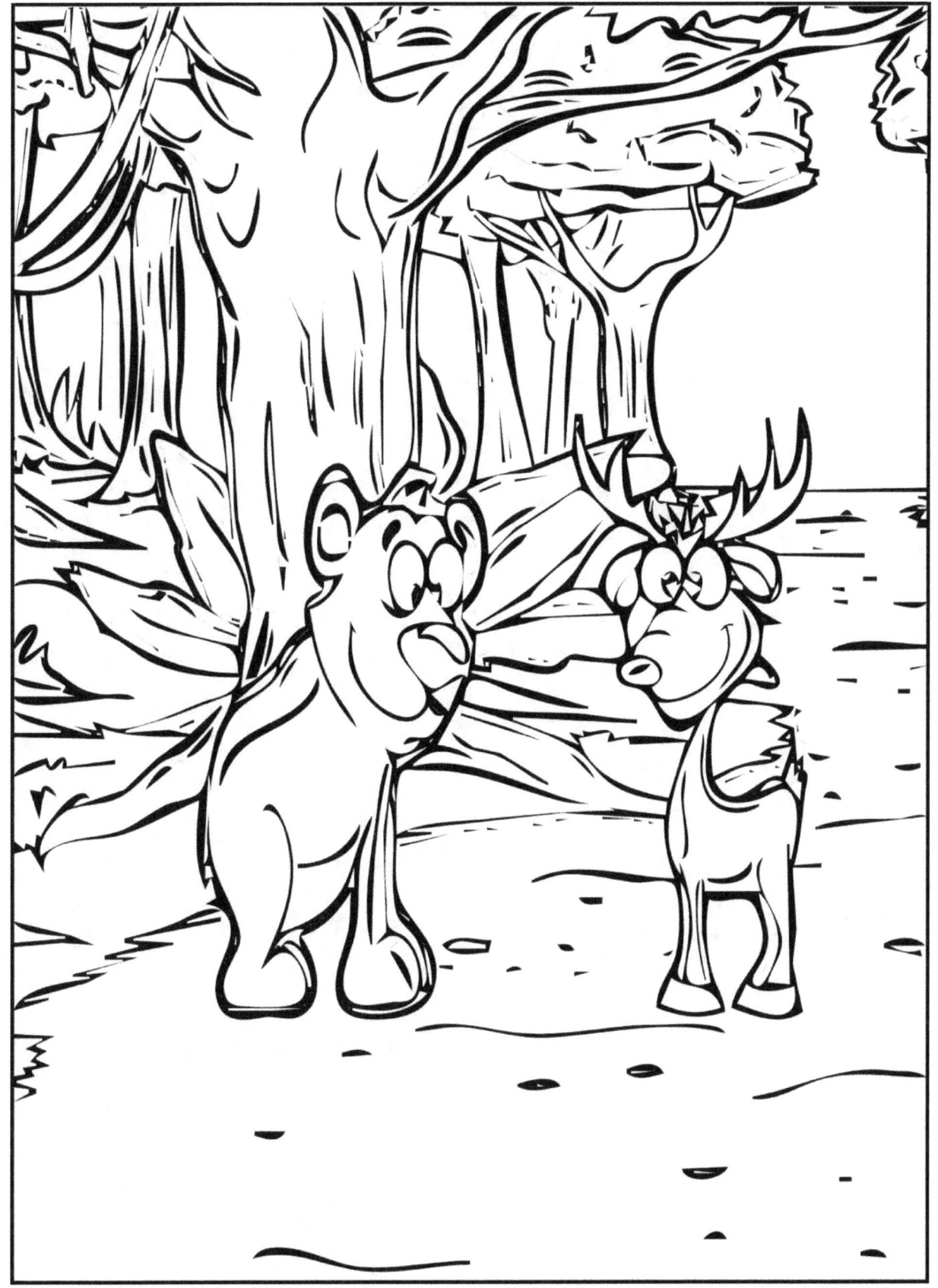

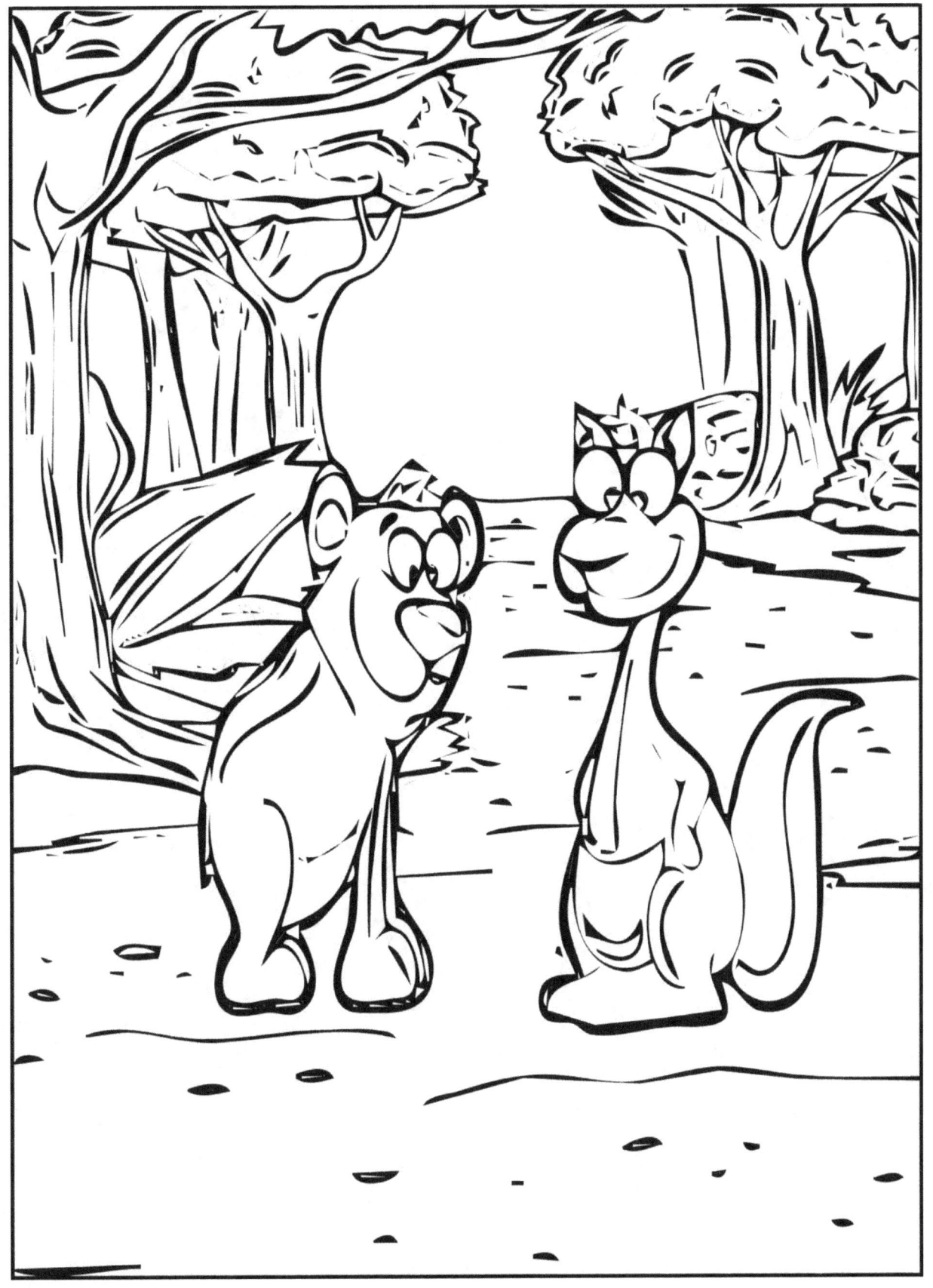

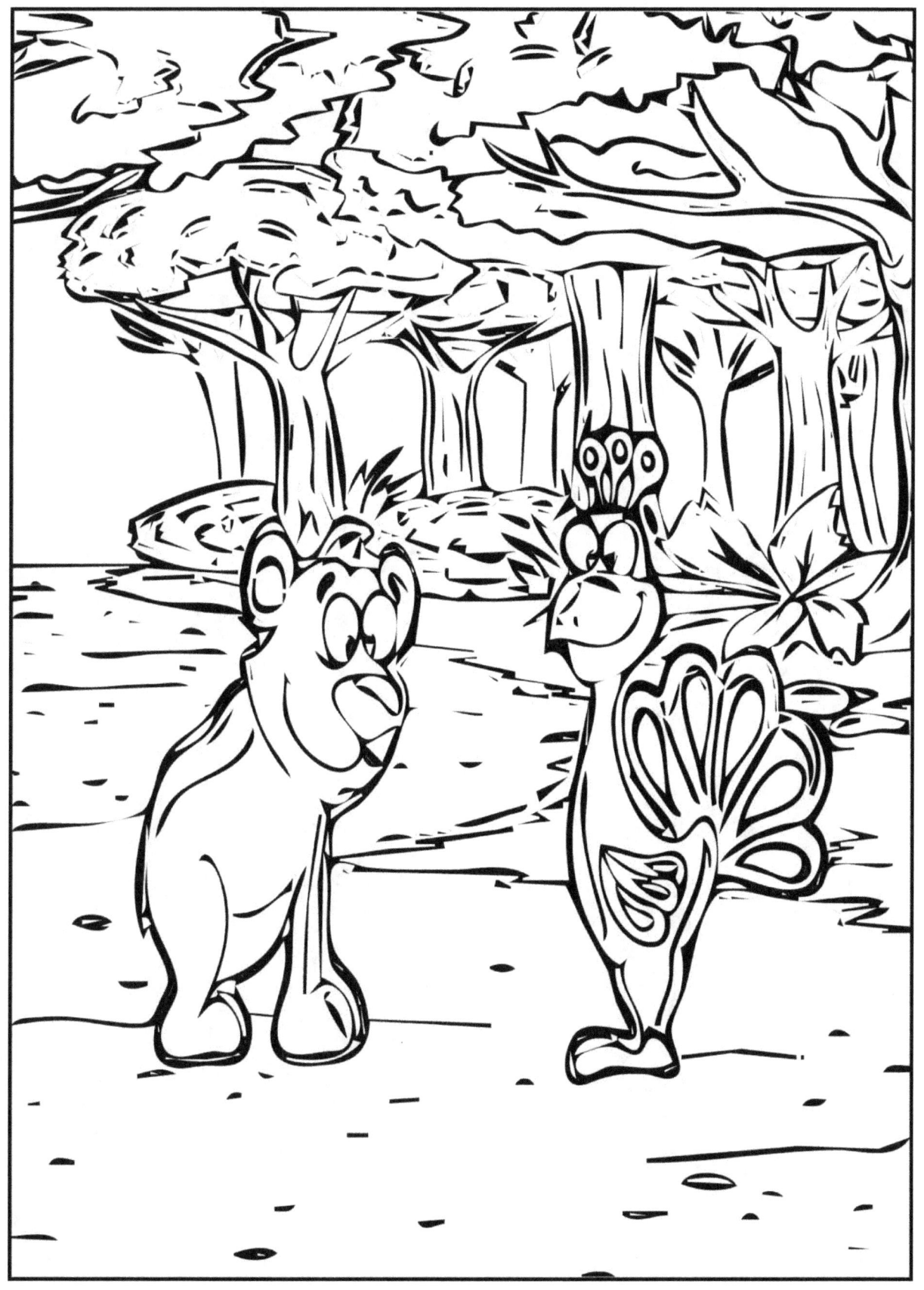

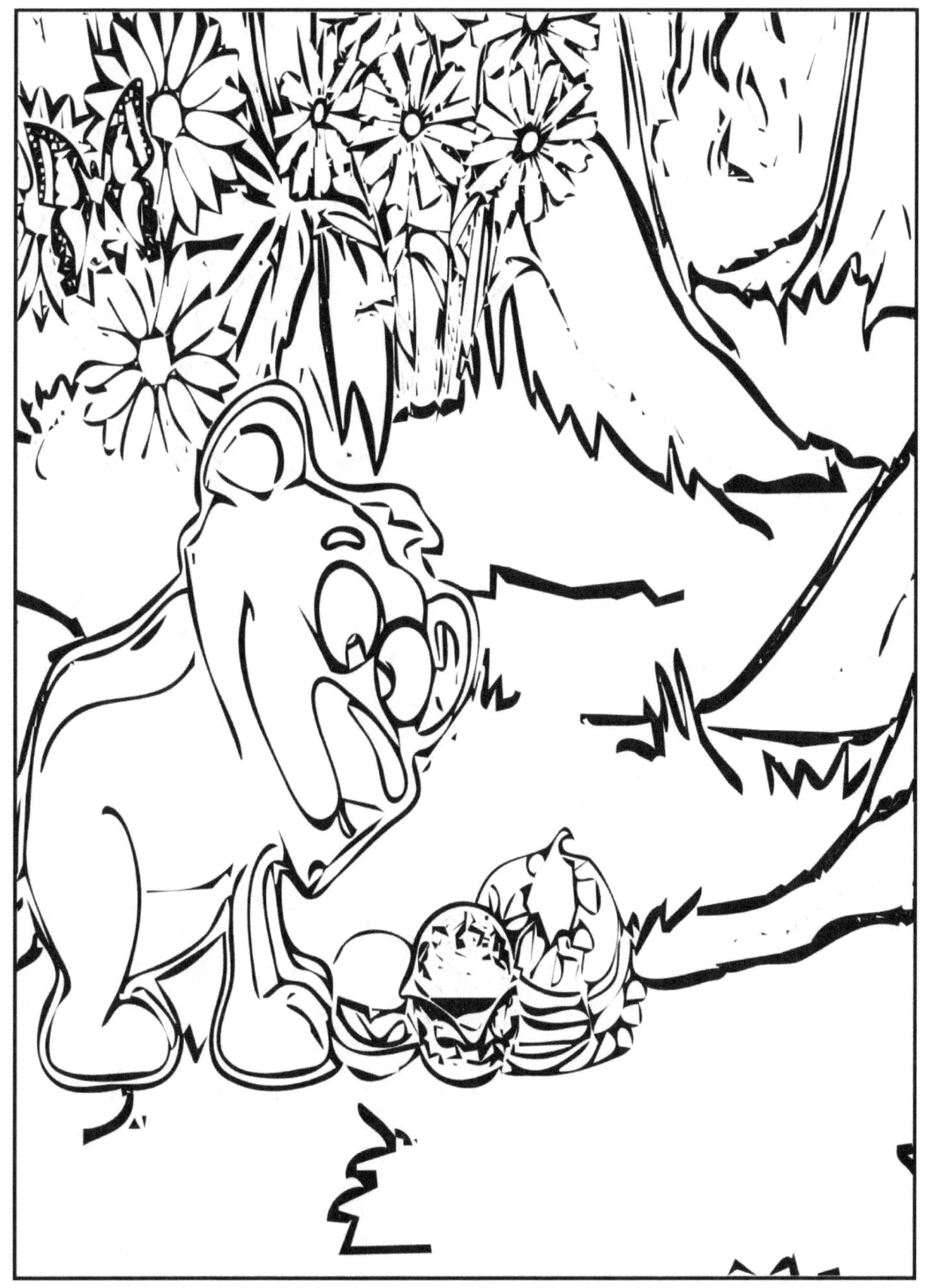

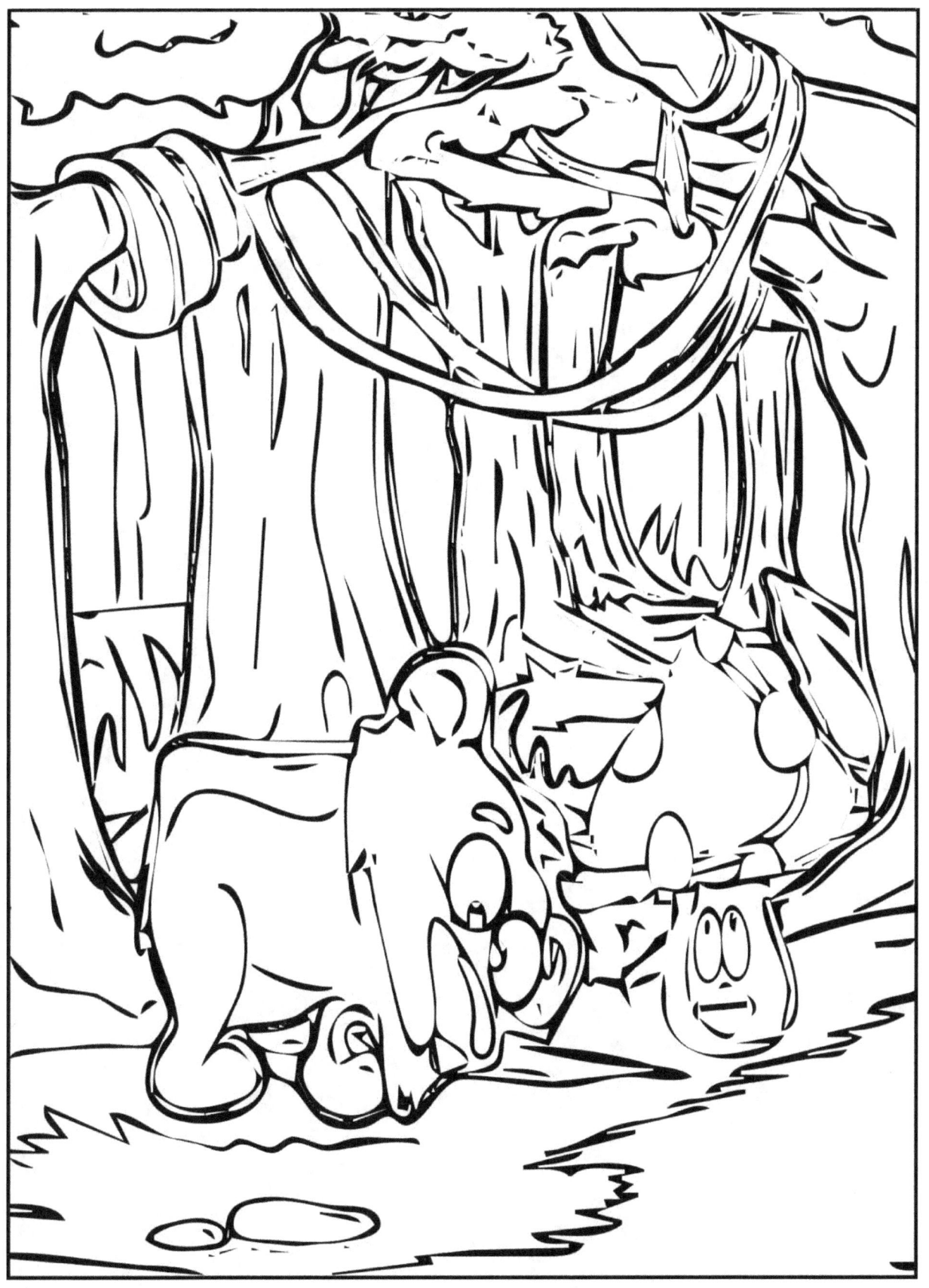

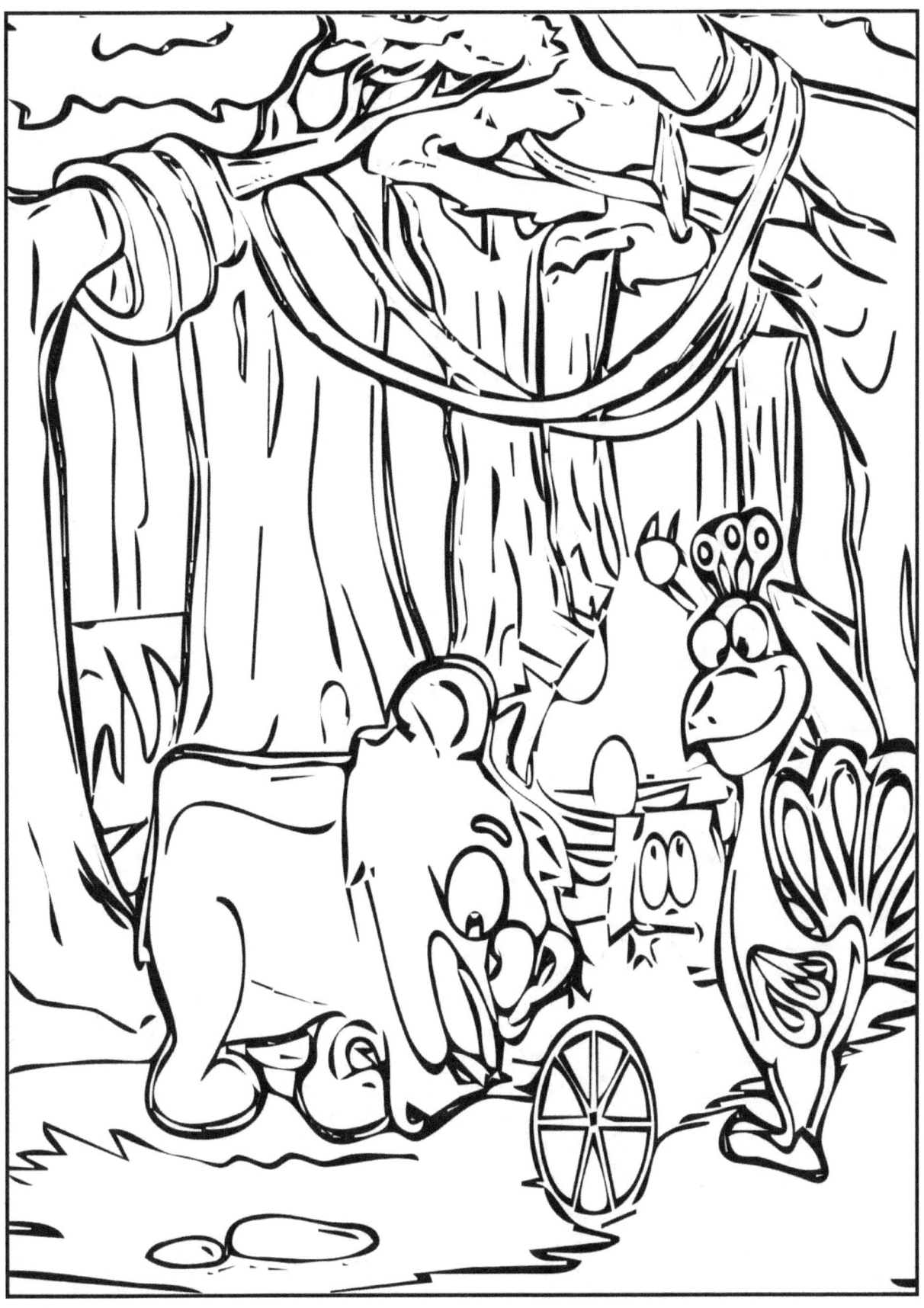

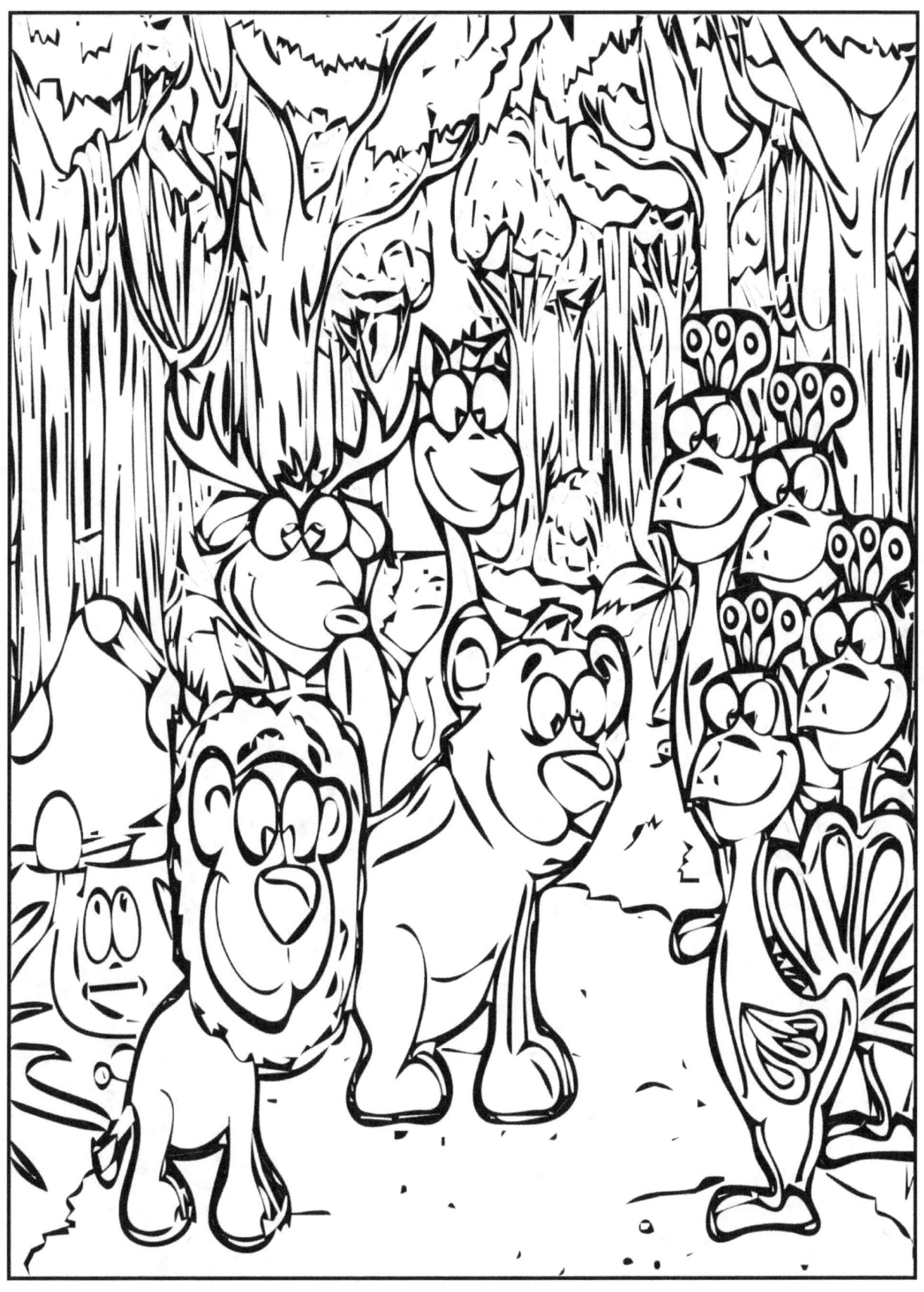

www.ingramcontent.com/pod-product-compliance
Lightning Source LLC
Chambersburg PA
CBHW081504170526
45166CB00008B/2541